Praise for *Educating Students Experiencing Homelessness, Instability, and Disengagement*

"Once again, Dr. Payne has created a practical, research-based resource for education practitioners to better understand and support our most vulnerable and misunderstood students."

—Dr. CJ Huff, co-founder,
Bright Futures USA, Springfield, Missouri

"As a former practitioner and principal in the public school system of Texas, I kept thinking to myself that this book would have been so beneficial to my staff of counselors, social workers, assistant principals, and teachers to help us cope with the students and families who entered our doors constantly. The book is timely and very much needed in our public schools."

—Dr. Billy Pringle, deputy director, Business Operations,
HS Services, Professional Development and Governance,
Texas Association of Secondary School Principals, Austin, Texas

"Dr. Payne presents a clear explanation of the current understanding of how the brain and nervous system affect learning, and most importantly, she provides immediately usable strategies for teachers."

—Claire Chumley, English teacher,
Barbers Hill High School, Mont Belvieu, Texas

"This information makes a huge difference in our work as administrators because it approaches relationships from a biological perspective and helps us to understand that responses we see from parents and students in conversations are often biological in nature and not controlled by conscious responses."

—Aaron Tomhave, assistant principal,
Keefer Crossing Middle School, New Caney, Texas

EDUCATING **STUDENTS** EXPERIENCING **HOMELESSNESS, INSTABILITY, AND DISENGAGEMENT**

The Impact of the
Autonomic Nervous System

RUBY K. PAYNE, PH.D.

Ruby K. Payne

Educating Students Experiencing Homelessness, Instability, and Disengagement: The Impact of the Autonomic Nervous System
116 pages
Bibliography: page 103
ISBN: 978-1-948244-62-6

aha! Process, Inc.
P.O. Box 727
Highlands, TX 77562-0727
(800) 424-9484 • (281) 426-5300
Fax: (281) 426-5600
www.ahaprocess.com

Cover and book design by Amy Alick Perich
Printed in White Plains, Maryland

Table of Contents

INTRODUCTION

This book is a why/how book. In other words, this is why this is happening (research), and this is how you can address it (strategy).

This book is for practitioners and is designed to be a quick read. It is a translation of the research so practitioners have tools for their realities.

Our current theories about how to educate are based upon a cognitive approach to learning, which basically ignores the neurobiology of the body. The neurobiology research has significantly increased in the last 20 years, bringing a different understanding of learning, as shown in the graphic on the next page.

Neurobiology model[1]

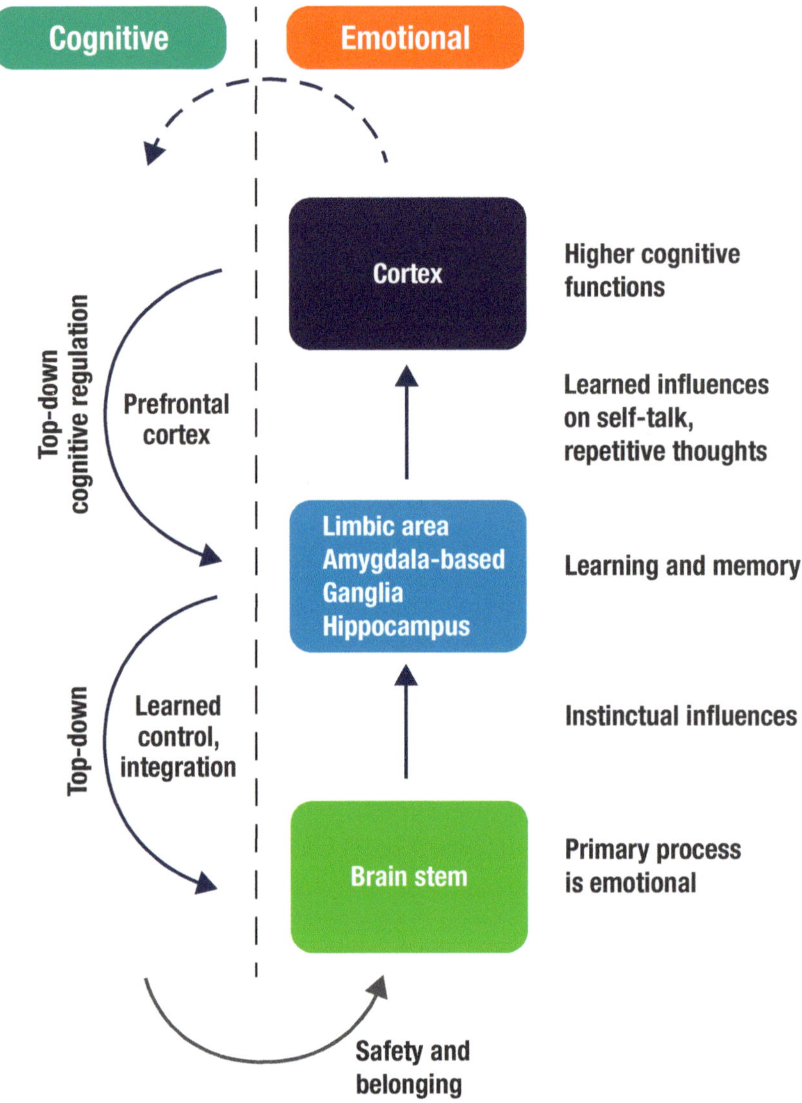

Adapted from "The Influences of Emotion on Learning and Memory."
www.frontiersin.org/articles/10.3389/fpsyg.2017.01454/full

As you can see in this simplified graphic, the right side of the chart shows emotional development, and the left side of the chart shows the cognitive development of the brain. Again, this chart is an oversimplification.

In the last 50 years, most of our educational approaches have been based on the left side of this chart. But we now know that in the first two years of life, the brain development tends to be focused on the right side of the brain (movement, sound, feelings, touch).

All emotional well-being and learning is based in safety and belonging. The only thing that is fully developed at birth is the brain stem. The primary process in the brain stem is about survival: *Is it safe? Do I belong? To what and to whom do I need to pay attention so I survive?* By the time you are three years old, much of your emotional self is established (amygdala). The amygdala and hippocampus are where memory and learning begin. The cortex is where language and conceptual frames are assigned. The prefrontal cortex then regulates and integrates those functions.

The development of the right side of the brain is critical for the functioning of the rest of the brain. Yet, in the education business, we ignore it. When students come to school from an environment where there is a great deal of instability, danger, war, trauma, etc., we do not know how to understand it or address their needs. Thus, we assign them to special education.

For a long time, we believed that the Earth was the center of the universe and that the Sun went around the Earth.

Then Copernicus came along and said, No, the Sun is the center of the universe and the Earth goes around the Sun. Copernicus was considered a heretic.

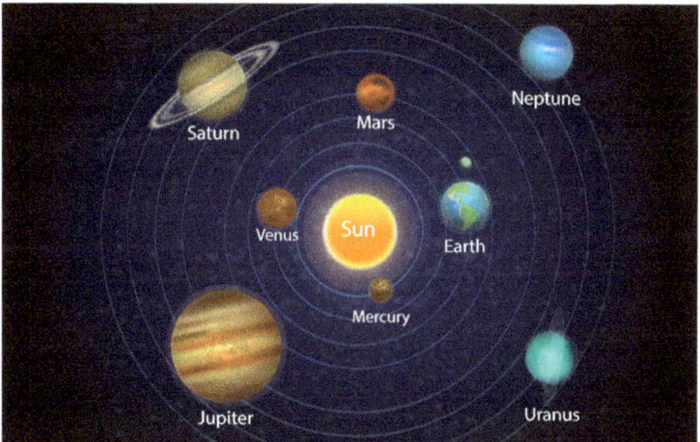

Right now our model of schooling is a model of collecting data, not necessarily of learning.

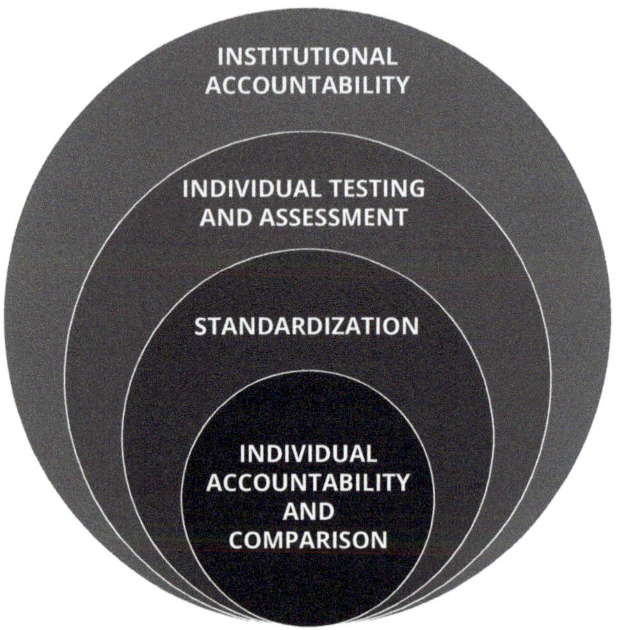

The results of this model have been 30% student disengagement, dropping test scores, 30% teacher disengagement, educators quitting, dropping achievement levels in multiple countries, more cheating at high schools and colleges, and 34% of adult males of working age who are not working.

This model gets higher achievement, higher engagement, and lower absenteeism.

Based on the neurobiology of the body, the model we could be using is the following:

How does it all fit together?

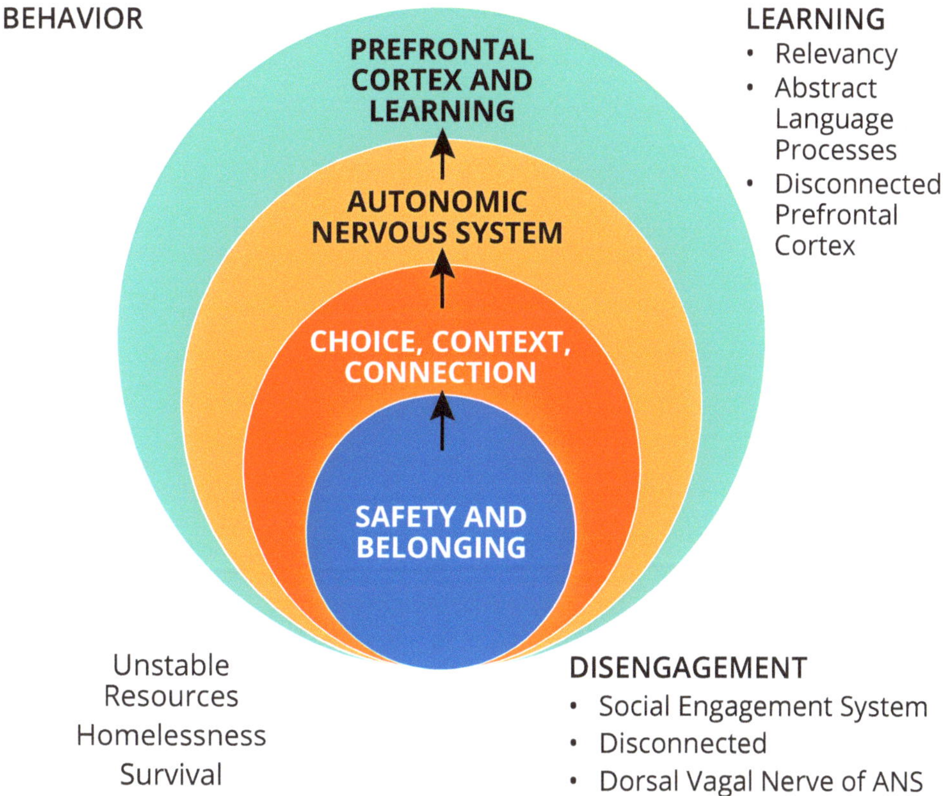

What this graphic means is that everything starts with safety and belonging. Safety and belonging is very dependent upon the choices we believe we have, the context (environment) we are in, and the connections we are able to make. It is about relevance, safety, and belonging. That leads to the status of the autonomic nervous system. Is it functioning in balance? If it is, then the prefrontal cortex is functioning, which leads to social engagement. Learning, engagement, and behavior is related to each part of the graphic.

How can we understand it better and get different outcomes?

This book will examine the research and the strategies to get there (why and how).

CHAPTER 1

WHY ARE STUDENTS DISENGAGED?

The Autonomic Nervous System

The body is an energy system

Your body is an energy system. If you have ever been in a room with an angry person, you can feel it. Waves from the heart go out three feet from the body. Acupuncture is based upon the energy system of your body.

Autonomic nervous system

Your responses are controlled by your autonomic nervous system (ANS).

- 99.99% of everything that happens in the body is under the control of the ANS. It happens automatically. We do not think about it.
- We have about five trillion bits of information coming into the brain every second, and we are only aware of about 10,000 bits.

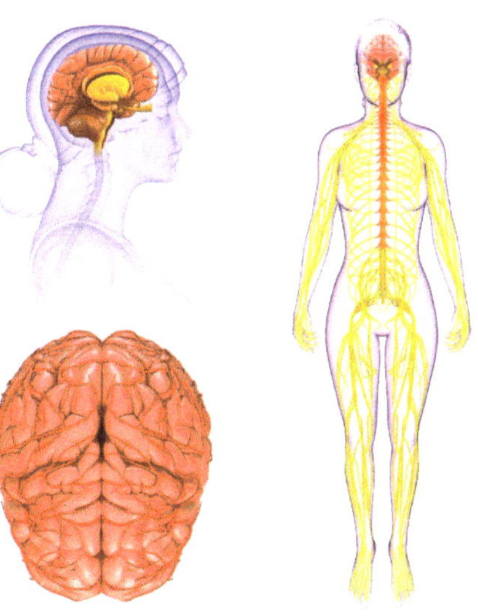

CANVA

The vagus nerve and your ANS

The vagus nerve is one of the longest nerves in the body and is part of the autonomic nervous system. It has two subsystems: the parasympathetic nervous system (PNS) and the sympathetic nervous system (SNS).

The parasympathetic nervous system is further divided into two subsections—one part above the diaphragm called the ventral vagal, and one part below the diaphragm called the dorsal vagal.

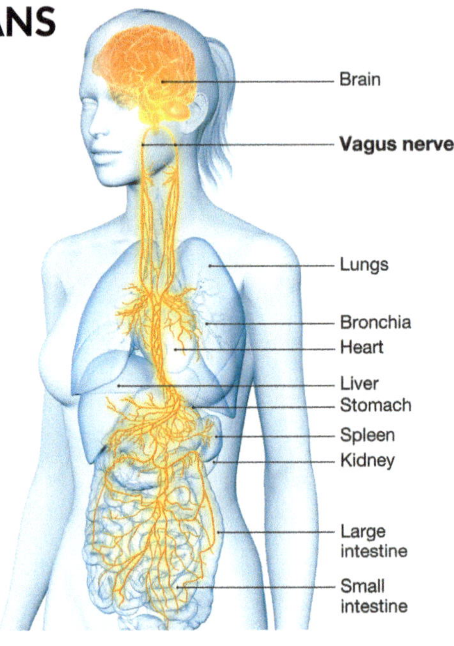

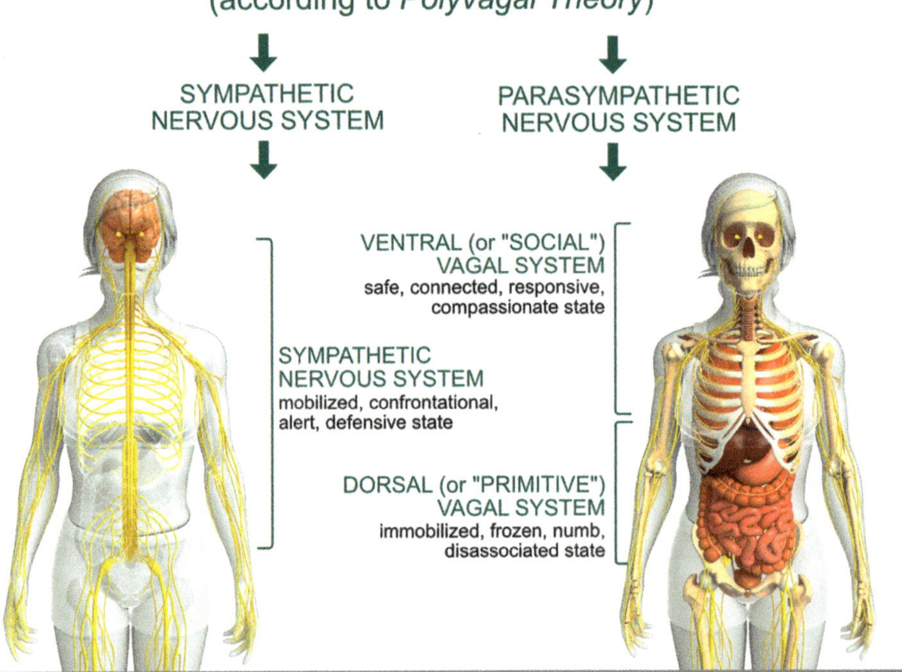

Adapted from Sequence Wiz

This system creates a hierarchy of responses based upon whether you think you are safe or not.

Ventral
(safe/connected)

- **Safely embodied**
- **Co-regulate**
- **Self-regulate**
- **Connect to others, the world, spirit**
- **Acknowledge distress**
- **Explore options**
- **Reach out for/offer support**
- **Resourced and resourceful**

Fight or Flight
SNS mobilized

- **Mobilize to survive**
- **Move into fight or flight**
- **Feel out of sync with others**
- **Driven to get needs met**
- **Alarmed, anxious**
- **Hypervigilant**
- **Misread cues**
- **Listen for sounds if danger**
- **Sacrifice social engagement for survival**

Dorsal Vagal

- **Withdraw**
- **Shut down**
- **Collapse**
- **Become foggy, numb**
- **Go through the motions**
- **Disconnect from self, others, the world, spirit**

Stephen Porges, author of *The Polyvagal Theory*, identifies the social engagement system as part of the ANS.[2] As you can see in this chart, there is a safe side and an unsafe side. On the unsafe side, your ANS system is making adaptations to perceived dangers. On the safe side, your ANS system is making adaptations to perceived safety.

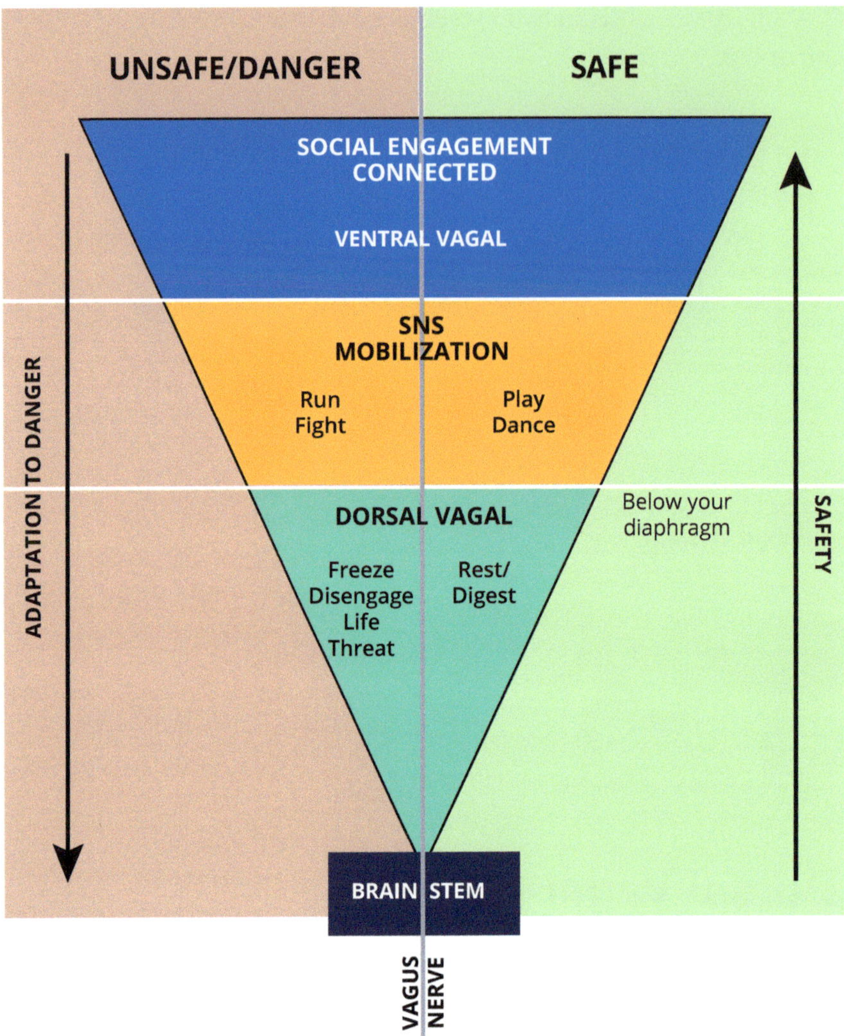

Why do people get stuck in the dorsal vagal (disengagement/sadness/ addiction)?

1. Repeated external circumstances where fighting/running does not work to keep you safe
2. Unsafe and dangerous adults or peers
3. Being bullied or shamed
4. Genetic predisposition to addiction, anxiety, autism, etc.; all of these things impact belonging
5. Absent/unavailable adults or the death of a key adult or peer
6. Consistently being found to be "less than" or "separate from"

7. A lack of spiritual support/belief; spiritual support/belief is linked in the research to high levels of resiliency and often (not always) to a safe support system that allows one to co-regulate
8. No future story
9. A series of unpredictable negative events over which one has no control (weather catastrophes, death, job loss, health issues, cancer, war, homelessness, etc.)
10. A lack of safety or belonging, either by the immediate acquaintances/family or the larger society
11. Fatigue

The social engagement system is tied to cranial nerves and blood flow and is connected to the heart. The heart has 60 times the electrical amplitude of the brain. (You have a "heart brain" and a "brain brain." If you have ever said something like, " I know it doesn't make sense but it feels right," your "heart brain" is in control.) This social engagement system reads the environment.

The heart (via the vagus nerve) and nerves in the face and head connect to control:

- Expression
- Hearing
- Spoken sound
- Voice tone
- Breathing
- Swallowing
- Head tilt
- Blood flow to lips
- Eyes
- Smell

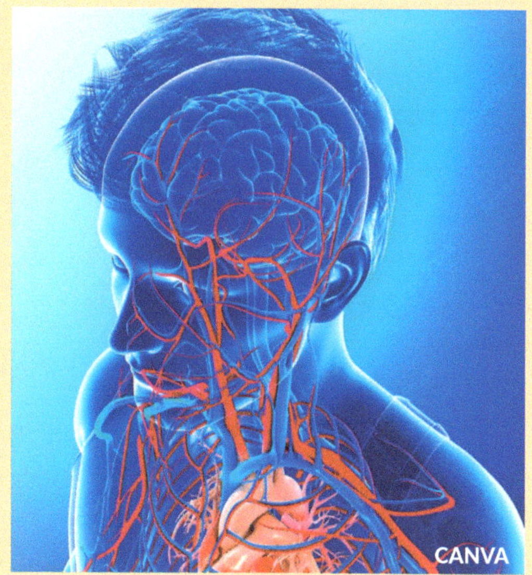

These all provide indicators of safety and belonging.

Social engagement initially always occurs in a dyad of two people—a mother and child, lovers, close friends. It is all from the nerves and blood flow that is connected to the heart. It is the first signal of safety and belonging.

Social engagement system

The social engagement system involves compassion. Compassion is the basis for desirable behavior.

Compassion...

- requires a lowering of defense systems.
- is incompatible with judgment, evaluation, or defensive behaviors and feelings.
- is a necessary part of co-regulation.
- is necessary for a sense of safety.

Three things your ANS does

In addition to the social engagement system, your ANS does three things:

Co-regulation is the initial subconscious reading of another person to assess safety and danger. You sync your energy with somebody else. Co-regulation initially occurs in dyads, one-on-one situations—for example, a mother and her infant.

Research from the HeartMath Institute, in which scientists measured heart waves, shows that when a dog and boy were together in the same room, their heartbeats were in sync. When they were put in separate rooms, their heartbeats were out of sync.[3]

Co-regulation is a key factor in safety and belonging. It is why you feel safe with a person and you don't necessarily know why. It just "feels" right.

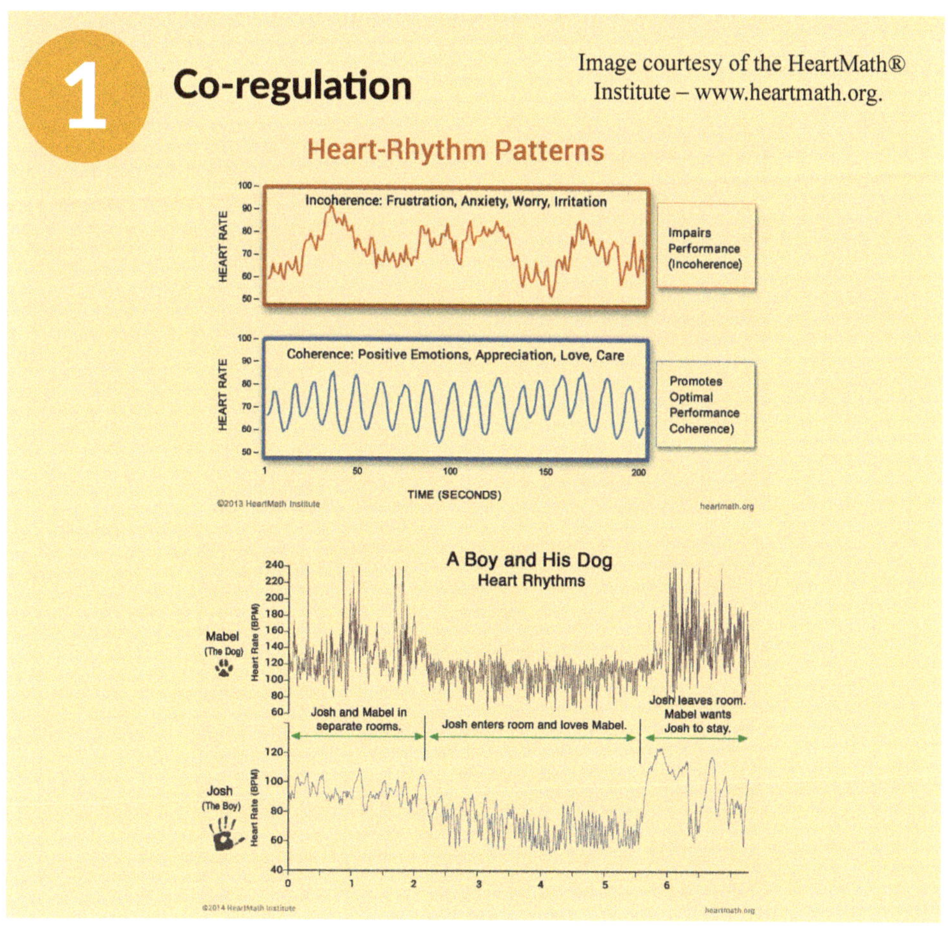

The second thing the ANS does is **neuroception.**

2

Neuroception

"Detection without awareness" —Porges

- ANS takes in information at the subconscious level.
- ANS responds to cues of safety and danger inside and outside the body. *Am I safe or not?*
- ANS brings the response to address the situation.

Mismatches/Misalignments

Inability to calm oneself in safe environments Hypervigilance	Inability to activate appropriate response in unsafe environments Unaware of risks taken

Neuroception is how your subconscious constantly reads the environment. It is below the level of awareness. If you have ever been in a space and felt uncomfortable, your neuroception was telling you that it sensed danger. Your ANS brings a response to the situation automatically without you having to think about it. Hypervigilance can occur if an individual has been in an unsafe environment for a long time. Often there is an inability to calm oneself even if an environment is safe. If you have been in a very protected environment, there may be an inability to activate an appropriate response or be aware of risks.

The third thing the ANS does is **operate in a hierarchy.**

This hierarchy has a safe side and an unsafe side. When individuals assess that their environment might not be safe, they will engage in negotiation, placating, trading, etc., to stay safe. If that does not work, they will go to mobilization (fight or run). If that also does not work, they will go to immobilization, withdrawal, freezing, or disengagement.

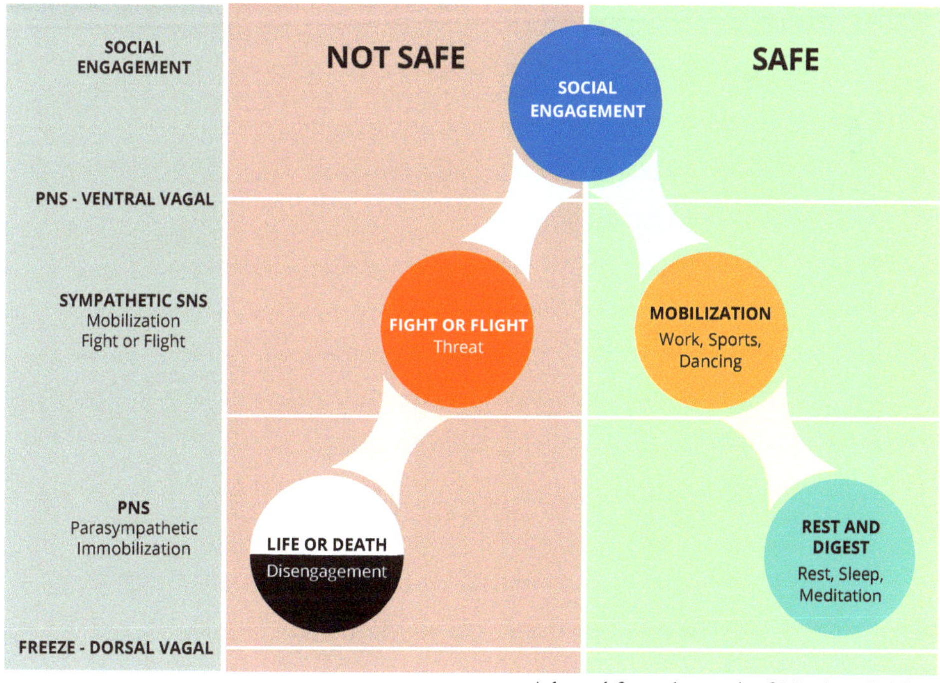

Adapted from the work of Matthew Tobias

An individual who is "healthy" will often move between the levels of the hierarchy. They tend to not get "stuck" in the dorsal vagal. For example, in part of one day, you may feel socially connected; in another part of that same day, you may be willing to fight for something; and in another part of that day, you may feel so discouraged that you just want to quit and hide.

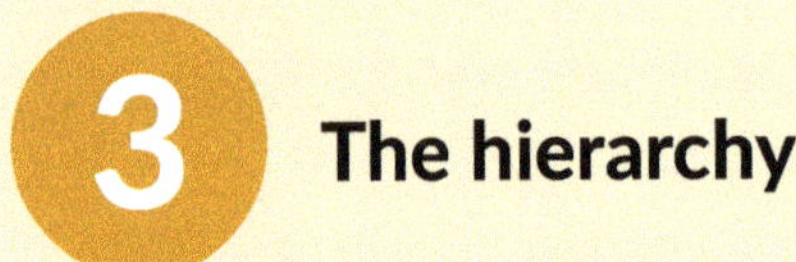

3 The hierarchy

Ventral
(safe/connected)

- Safely embodied
- Co-regulate
- Self-regulate
- Connect to others, the world, spirit
- Acknowledge distress
- Explore options
- Reach out for/offer support
- Resourced and resourceful

Fight or Flight
SNS mobilized

- Mobilize to survive
- Move into fight or flight
- Feel out of sync with others
- Driven to get needs met
- Alarmed, anxious
- Hypervigilant
- Misread cues
- Listen for sounds if danger
- Sacrifice social engagement for survival

Dorsal Vagal

- Withdraw
- Shut down
- Collapse
- Become foggy, numb
- Go through the motions
- Disconnect from self, others, the world, spirit

If I am in an environment where there is not safety and belonging, and if negotiation, fighting, or running do not work, then I will disengage, freeze, withdraw, become addicted, become suicidal, etc. I will not participate.

This situation then becomes even more exacerbated if there is a comparison because it changes the story of who I am. Deb Dana, in her book *Polyvagal Flip Chart: Understanding the Science of Safety*, identifies this process. The process indicates that as you move from connection to protection to disengagement, the story in your head about yourself changes.[4]

What comparison does to your story

PNS Ventral ANS Above Diaphragm	SNS	PNS Dorsal Below Diaphragm
STORY OF CONNECTION	STORY OF PROTECTION	STORY OF DISENGAGEMENT
Connected Cooperate Positive self-talk Compassion for others	Competition Judgment Critical of others	No hope Negative self-talk Critical of others
I wonder... I am curious... I want to know more...	I have to be the best or at least better than others	I will never be good enough
Social engagement Health Growth Regulated brain	Protection through action	Protection by disappearing Save energy and resources

Safety and belonging

If I am connected, I have safety and belonging, I am curious, I wonder, and I want to know more. My story is one of connection.

If I am in competition, comparison, or judgment, I believe that I must be the best or better than others. My story is one of protection.

If I believe that I will never be good enough, then my story is one of disengagement.

Your safety and belonging are further impacted by context, choice, and connection.

ANS is impacted by

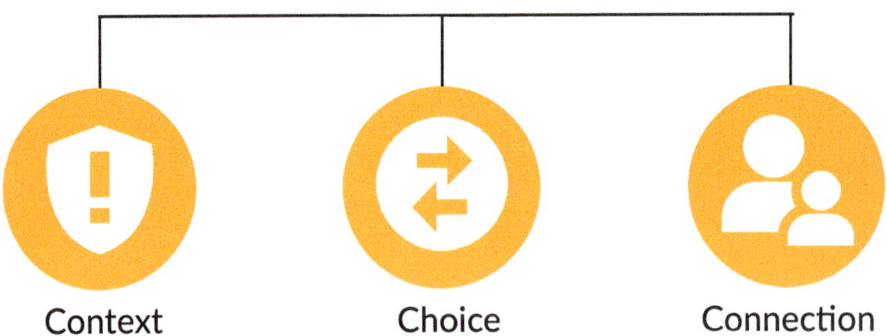

This impacts how much safety or belonging you think you have.

This impacts the story you carry in your head about yourself.

What are the strategies to address disengagement?

STRATEGY ONE

1. **To build co-regulation, there is a neurolinguistic programming technique called mirroring.** In this strategy, you match your verb choice to someone else's verb choice, and you "mirror" their body.

STRATEGY TWO

2. **To move someone from disengagement to connection,** the process outlined below is very helpful.

People can take multiple steps to move from disengagement to connection.

Step one: no energy / low energy

- Acknowledge your feelings.
- Identify your negative self-talk (use if/then to identify the validity of self-talk).
- Give permission to your reality.
- Identify one small thing that you could do differently physically.

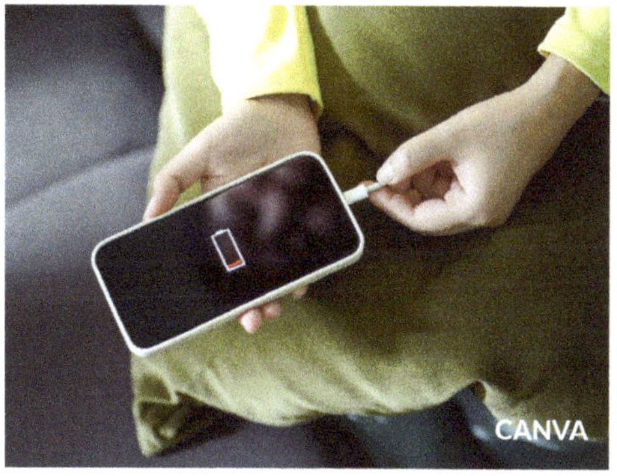

Step two: the "reconnecting" stage

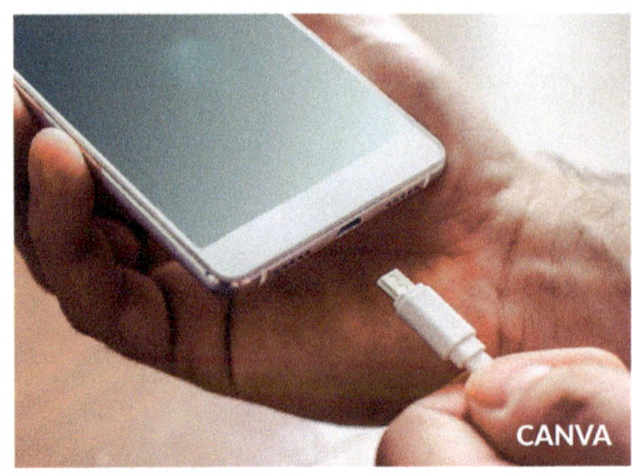

- Reconnect to safety. Identify your safety anchors, including people, pets, and places.
- Identify who your toxic co-authors are.
- Reconnect to environments. Connect with calming external environments (nature, music).

Step three: the "return of energy" stage—moving to mobilization

- Increase the vagal brake strength (influence of safety on your heart) that you will need to employ.
- Be prepared for discomfort while your autonomic nervous system adjusts to sharing space without running or fighting.
- You will feel a need to run or fight (you are now moving into the sympathetic nervous system). Because of the anxiety that can be created, there is often a return to self-soothing behaviors (addictions, etc.).
- Typically, the fight stage (irritability, anger) comes before the run stage. Dysregulated anger operates out of fear. Translate the fight into a way to have more personal power while you have healthy boundaries.
- It helps in this stage if there is a movement into play, which is the safe side of mobilization.

Step four: moving to connection, activating the social engagement system

- Basic social engagement is a dyad involving one other person.
- Find one other person you can interact with over a shared interest or a common bond. If it is comfortable, find a group to be a part of.

- The social engagement system is the relationship between the brain stem, the cranial nerves, and the blood flow into the face.
- The face–heart connection is:
  a. Speaking to the heart (e.g., chanting, singing).
  b. Listening to the heart (e.g., listening to music).
  c. Breathing with the heart (connecting with the heart).
- The posture–heart connection is dancing and other movement.
- These connections change the response of the autonomic nervous system.

STRATEGY THREE

Development of compassion (the basis of desirable behavior)...

- requires a lowering of defense systems.
- is incompatible with judgment, evaluation, or defensive behaviors and feelings.
- is a necessary part of co-regulation.
- is necessary for a sense of safety.
- allows for social engagement without fear.

CANVA

When there is not social engagement, the face becomes "flat" and expressionless.

To develop compassion, it is important to see the situation from the other person's perspective.

Questions to ask include: How do you think the other person thought about this? Why might they have done that?

STRATEGY FOUR

Stephen Porges recommends these strategies to move up the hierarchy:

1. Kazoo—allows you to breathe slowly.
2. Top down—think of a loving connection.
3. Rub your forehead—connects to your brain stem and the vagal nerve.
4. Rub your neck—close to the brain stem.
5. Rock your body from side to side or from front to back.[5]

STRATEGY FIVE

Other research recommends the following:

- Tapping—resets the autonomic nervous system.
- Standing straight with good posture—puts more oxygen into the autonomic nervous system and tends to calm you down.
- Looking up—the neurology of the brain processes visual information; when you look down, the brain tends to process emotional information.
- Water—metabolizes cortisol and lessens anxiety.

STRATEGY SIX

Accountability and testing involve comparisons. Both the military and sports teams are very competitive and have a great deal of comparisons. What they both do is to make sure there is belonging, that they are a part of a team. Universities understand that the completion rates in graduate school significantly improve if adults are part of a cohort, and they intentionally create social events to improve the belonging in a cohort.

a. I know a high school chemistry teacher who had his students in teams of four. On Monday, he lectured. On Tuesday and Wednesday, the teams worked in the lab. On Thursday, the teams studied for the test. On Friday, they took the test. He told his students that if everyone on their team got a 70 or better on the test on Friday, he would add five additional points to each person's individual grade. The groups then became so competitive that he made this rule: If everyone in the class got a 70 or better, he would add 10 additional points to each individual grade. His goal was to improve learning for everyone.

b. At elementary school, you assign buddies for recess and lunch. No one plays alone or eats alone.

c. At middle school, a seventh-grade teacher made a football field on the wall of his classroom. Students were in teams of two, and they selected a football team from a college/university they were interested in. He grouped them into NFL and AFL leagues. Then he posted on the wall a list—this is how you gain yards (behaviors he wanted), this is how you lose yards (behaviors he did not want), and this how you make a touchdown. The footballs moved during the week, and there were competitions and prizes.

STRATEGY SEVEN

To change stories, use a metaphor story. Another technique for working with students and adults is to use metaphor stories. A metaphor story will help an individual voice issues that affect subsequent actions. A metaphor story doesn't have any proper names in it.

For example, Jennifer, a student, keeps going to the nurse's office two or three times a week. There is nothing wrong with her. Yet she keeps going. An adult says to her, "Jennifer, I am going to tell a story, and I need you to help me. It's about a fourth-grade girl much like yourself. I need you to help me tell the story because I'm not in fourth grade."

> *"Once upon a time there was a girl who went to the nurse's office. Why did the girl go to the nurse's office? (Because she thought there was something wrong with her.) The girl went to the nurse's office because she thought there was something wrong with her. Did the nurse find anything wrong with her? (No, the nurse did not.) The nurse didn't find anything wrong with her, yet the girl kept going to the nurse. Why did the girl keep going to the nurse? (Because she thought there was something wrong with her.) So, the girl thought something was wrong with her. Why did the girl think there was something wrong with her? (She saw a TV show...)"*

The story continues until the reason for the behavior is found, and then the story needs to end on a positive note: *"She went to the doctor, and the doctor gave her tests and found that she was okay."*

This is an actual case. What came out in the story was that Jennifer had seen a TV show in which a girl her age had died suddenly and had never known she was ill. Jennifer's parents took her to the doctor, and the doctor ran tests and told Jennifer she was fine. After that, she didn't go to the nurse's office anymore.

A metaphor story is to be used one-on-one when there is a need to understand the existing behavior and motivate the student to implement the appropriate behavior.[6]

STRATEGY EIGHT

At middle school, use information from www.beyonddifferences.org/social-isolation to engage students at lunch. The curriculum is free.

Summary

1. Your body is an energy system.
2. Your autonomic nervous system (ANS) controls most of your responses.
3. Your ANS responds to the context and impacts your story.
4. Your ANS does three things: co-regulation, neuroception, and operating in a hierarchy.
5. You can have a story of connection, protection, or disengagement.
6. Comparison often makes your story one of protection or disengagement.
7. Context, choice, and connection impact your ANS.

CHAPTER 2

THE AUTONOMIC NERVOUS SYSTEM AND LEARNING

Learning

When a person is in the SNS (fight or flight) or the dorsal vagal, their prefrontal cortex is partially or totally disabled, and it is difficult to think, particularly abstractly. And if the information has no emotional significance at a personal level, the information is often not learned (context, choice, connection). Many people have heard the phrase "rigor, relationships, relevance." State assessment has standards for rigor, but there are no standards for relevance.

Ventral
(safe/connected)

Prefrontal cortex is working.

Student can self-regulate, learn, use language to negotiate.

Fight or Flight
SNS mobilized

Prefrontal cortex is disabled.

Amygdala is in charge. Learning is reduced. Anger, irritation is increased. Will "run" from tasks.

Dorsal Vagal

Prefrontal cortex is disabled.

Student is immobilized. Shuts down. Disengagement. Little to no learning.

If you are in the SNS or the dorsal vagal, the ability to learn is significantly reduced. There are several factors why. First of all, the allostatic load in your brain is higher. Stress, which is allostatic load, will further reduce the amount of information that can be processed to about one or two pieces of information.

Working memory

The prefrontal cortex and learning

When learning occurs, it goes to working memory in the prefrontal cortex. Working memory is like a longneck beer bottle—it limits what can get into the brain to four or five pieces of information. When it is overloaded, it shuts off any new information within 12 seconds. And if that information is not revisited within 24 hours, it is lost.

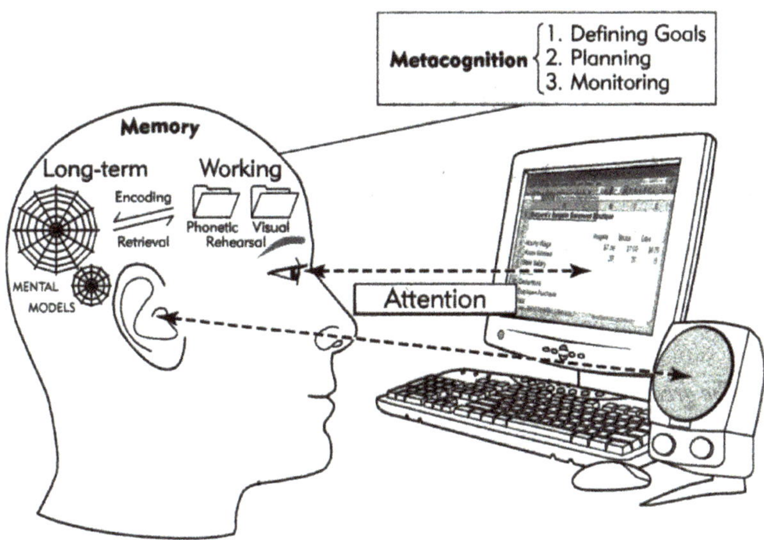

Source: *Building Expertise: Cognitive Methods for Training and Performance* (pp. 50–51) by R. C. Clark, 2008, San Francisco: Pfeiffer. Copyright 2008 by John Wiley & Sons. Reprinted with permission.

As you can see in the preceding graphic, working memory takes in information in two main channels: auditory and visual. When we ask students who are new to the information we are providing to use a third channel, the information dropouts start. For example, if the teacher is lecturing (auditory) and using a slide presentation (visual) and asks a student to take notes (kinesthetic), a student for whom this is new learning will not be able to absorb it all and will start losing information. It is much better to have the students listen to the lecture and see the presentation. After the presentation, give them the notes, and have them work with a partner to highlight the notes.

Ruth Colvin Clark, in her book *Building Expertise: Cognitive Methods for Training and Performance Improvement*, indicates that these are the eight pieces you must have for lesson design to get information into long-term memory:

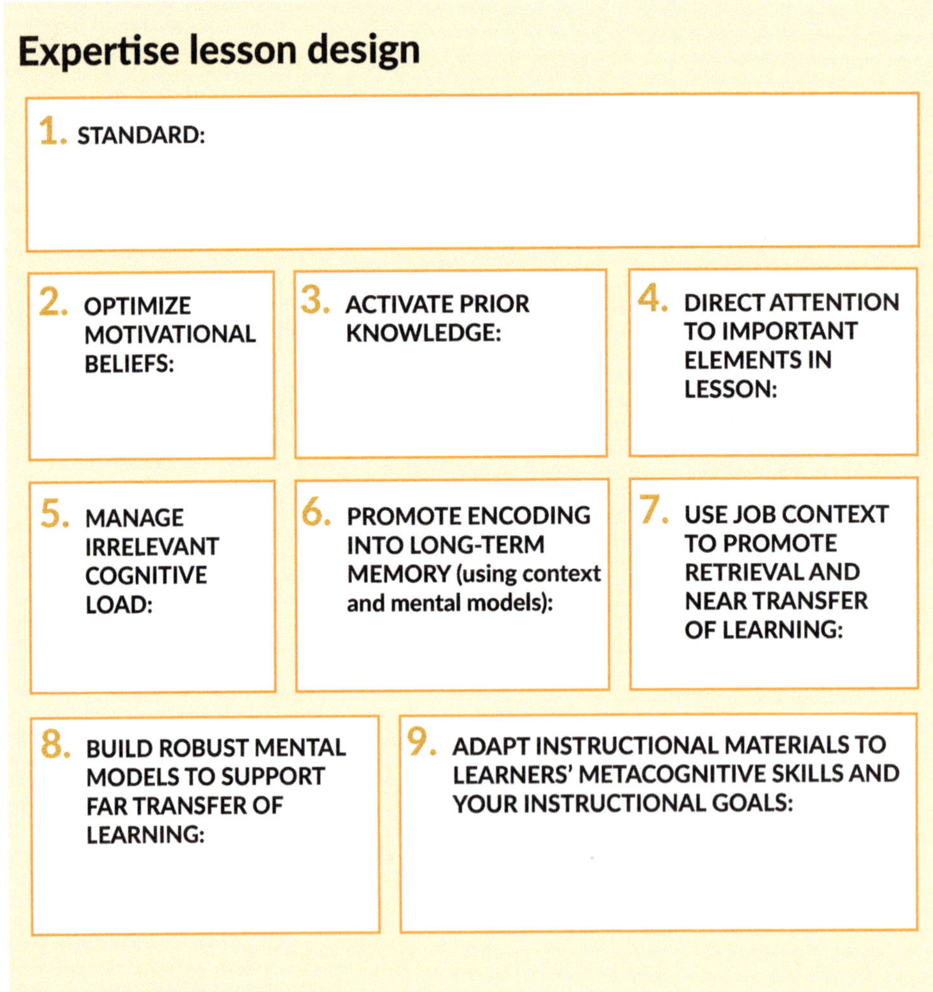

In other words, what the student must do is: (1) know what they are going to learn, (2) believe this is something they can learn or that it has value for them, (3) identify what they already know about it, (4) know what the important elements in the learning are, (5) manage their irrelevant cognitive load (all of the things that they are thinking/worried about that are not related to the learning), (6) use mental models (stories, analogies, or drawings) to translate from abstract to concrete, (7) identify job context (in other words, *How will I use this in the future?*), and (8) build their own mental model to remember the information. The teacher then adapts the materials to achieve long-term instructional goals.[7]

Relevance: The emotional connection

One of the huge issues for students today is that there is little relevance in the information. The information is presented abstractly, separate from the concrete, sensory reality of "real life."

State assessments have criteria for rigor but none for relevance.

Relevance comes in learning because the individual has an interest in the topic, has an emotional connection to the topic, knows someone who is involved with the topic, or senses that that the topic is tied to a concrete reality that he or she is involved with. An analogy would be to teach thermodynamics to someone who wants to be artist. There is no connection. For example, I know an Algebra I teacher who taught algebra by having the students bring in their cell phone bills. She taught them how to use algebra to predict their bills.

- You have to teach students to plan (build executive function) because the prefrontal cortex is not as developed.
- Visual images (mental models) can be used to translate new ideas to the concrete. Visual imaging capability is not affected by poverty. Because the hippocampus is not as developed for learning and memory, visuals help students learn.
- Vocabulary acquisition can be taught by using sketching, a visual activity.
- Procedural processes must be taught (these build executive function in the prefrontal cortex). Details can be managed using visuals and step sheets.
- Well-organized, non-chaotic schools and classrooms reduce allostatic load. Classroom management is a must because it allows working memory to function better.

- Link reward systems to planning by giving rewards to recognize completion of a plan. This helps develop the prefrontal cortex.
- Use visuals to translate from the concrete sensory world to the abstract representational world of paper, ideas, numbers, letters, drawings, etc.
- Question making helps students deal with nonroutine tasks and problem-solving (builds executive function).
- There will be more behavioral issues in poverty because of the larger amygdala and smaller hippocampus. Regulation of behavior must be taught.
- The role of nurturance—relationships—in the modulation of allostatic load and gene expression is important in learning.
- You have to manage the irrelevant working memory load. Working memory is like the neck of a bottle in that it limits what can get into the brain—usually about four to five pieces of new information at one time. When working memory gets overloaded, it shuts off any new information within 12 seconds. Stress (allostatic load) will further reduce the amount down to one or two pieces of information at a time.

Summary

1. When you are in SNS (fight or flight) or the dorsal vagal, the prefrontal cortex is disabled and learning is significantly reduced.
2. When the allostatic load is high (SNS or dorsal vagal), the "bandwidth" of the brain is significantly reduced and learning is reduced.
3. To get to long-term memory from working memory requires mental models and relevance.
4. Safety and belonging significantly increase learning.

CHAPTER 3

THE AUTONOMIC NERVOUS SYSTEM AND BEHAVIOR

A great number of discipline referrals tend to come when students are in the SNS. When they are in the dorsal vagal, they are disengaged, may have an addiction, and often suffer from a great deal of anxiety.

ANS hierarchy

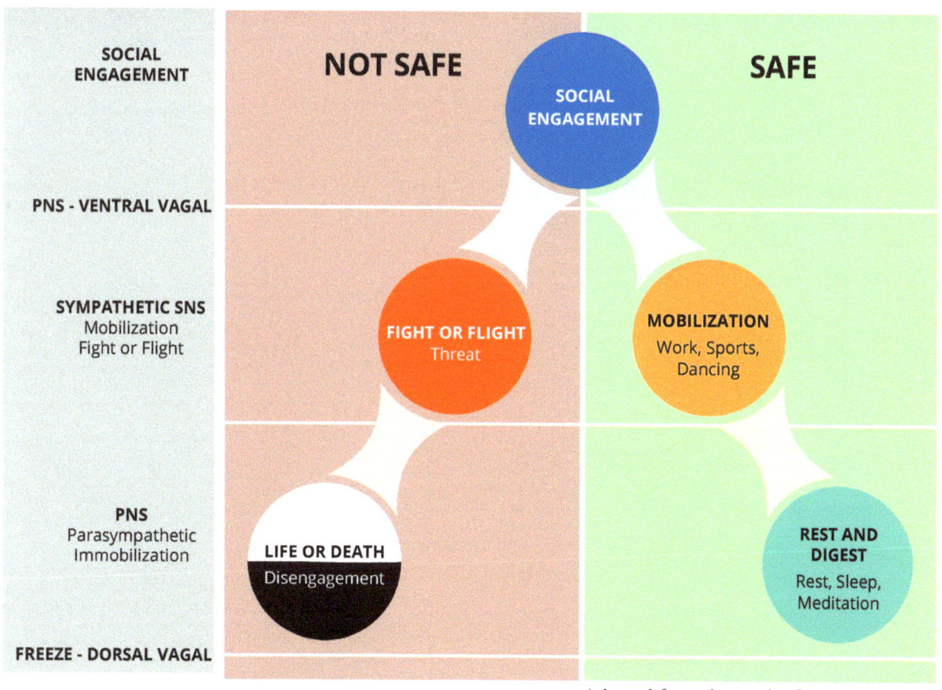

Adapted from the work of Matthew Tobias

It should be noted that almost all discipline issues arise on the unsafe side of the chart.

Where does the understanding of the brain, ANS, and behavior come together?

To better understand the relationship with the ANS and behavior, it is important to have some basics about how the brain functions.

The hand model

To understand the basic structure of the brain, the "hand model," as explained by Daniel Siegel, is very helpful.

The palm represents the brain stem, where the ANS originates.

The wrist represents the spinal cord. The vagus nerve goes down the spinal cord and connects the organs and systems of the body. This becomes the ANS.

The brain stem...

- controls our states of arousal—hunger, sexual, awake, asleep.
- is responsible for fight-or-flight response.
- identifies how we respond to threats; in survival mode, brain becomes reactive.
- is fundamental to motivational systems that help us with food, shelter, reproduction, and safety.
- works with the limbic area to get us to act.

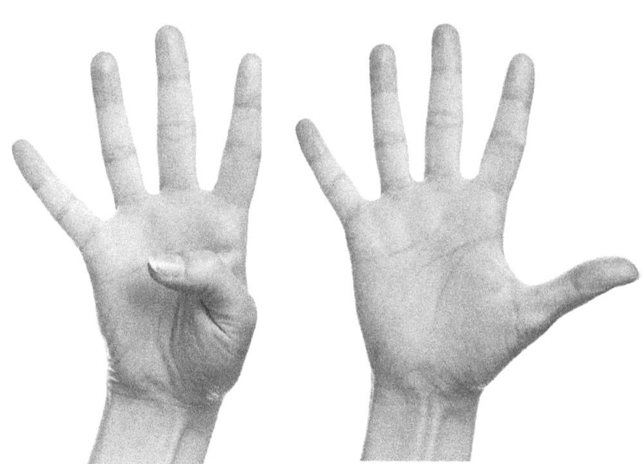

The thumb represents the limbic region of the brain. It is the amygdala, which is surrounded by the hippocampus.

Emotion

The limbic area (includes amygdala and hippocampus):

- Works with the brain stem to create our emotions
- Evaluates the situation—good (compassionate) or bad (uncompassionate)? We move toward the good and away from the bad
- Creates "e-motions"—the motion we choose (toward or away from), according to the meaning we assign to the situation
- Is crucial to how we form relationships and become emotionally attached to one another
- Regulates the hypothalamus, which is the endocrine control center; when we are stressed, we secrete a hormone that stimulates the adrenal glands to release cortisol, which mobilizes energy by putting our entire system on alert
- Is sensitized by trauma and then overfires; "finding a way to soothe excessively reactive limbic firing is crucial to rebalancing emotions and diminishing the harmful effects of chronic stress"[8]
- Helps create memories—of facts, experiences, emotions
- Includes the amygdala, which is especially important in the fear response; "emotional responses can be created without consciousness and we may act on them without awareness"[9]
- Includes the hippocampus, which puts the puzzle pieces together; i.e., it is responsible for the integration of experiences—body sensations, emotions, thoughts, facts, recollections, etc.
- As we age, "the hippocampus weaves the basic forms of emotional and perceptual memory into factual and autobiographical recollections"[10]

The cortex

The back of the hand and the fingers over the thumb represent the cortex of the brain.

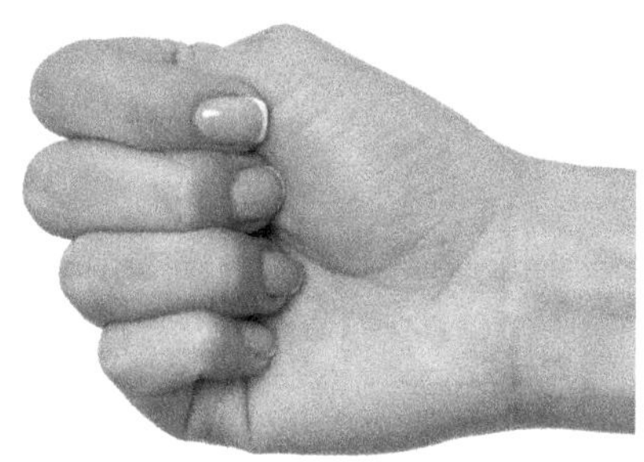

The cortex:

- Is the outer layer of the brain
- The frontal cortex moves the brain beyond survival, bodily functions, and emotional reactions and into thoughts and ideas
- The frontal cortex creates its own representations—it allows us to think about thinking
- In the hand model of the brain, the frontal cortex extends from your fingertips to the second knuckle

Prefrontal cortex

The middle two fingers are the prefrontal cortex.

Adapted from D. J. Siegel, *Mindsight*

The prefrontal cortex:

- In the hand model of the brain, the prefrontal cortex extends from your first knuckle to your fingertips
- Develops a sense of time, a sense of self, and moral judgments
- In the hand model of the brain, the two middle fingers are the middle prefrontal region—it controls impulsivity, has insight and empathy, and enacts moral judgments
- Because the prefrontal cortex is not well-developed in poverty,[11] "the nine prefrontal functions: (1) bodily regulation, (2) attuned communication, (3) emotional balance, (4) response flexibility, (5) fear modulation, (6) empathy, (7) insight, (8) moral awareness, and (9) intuition"[12] are also underdeveloped

Put your thumb in the middle of your palm, and curl your fingers over the top. The back of the hand represents the back of your head. Your wrist is the spinal cord rising from your backbone, upon which your brain sits. The inner brain stem is your palm. Your thumb in your palm represents the limbic region of the brain. Your fingers curled over the top of your thumb represent your cortex.

The brain stem, the limbic area, and the cortex are what have been called "the triune brain." To integrate the brain means linking the activities of the brain stem, the limbic area, and the cortex. It means that these parts "talk" to each other. This is called vertical integration.

If I believe I am in danger and my brain is wired (has experienced it many times) as unsafe, then I will often explode. The amygdala will disable the prefrontal cortex. The prefrontal cortex regulates and integrates brain responses. So when it is disabled, brain responses are often explosions.

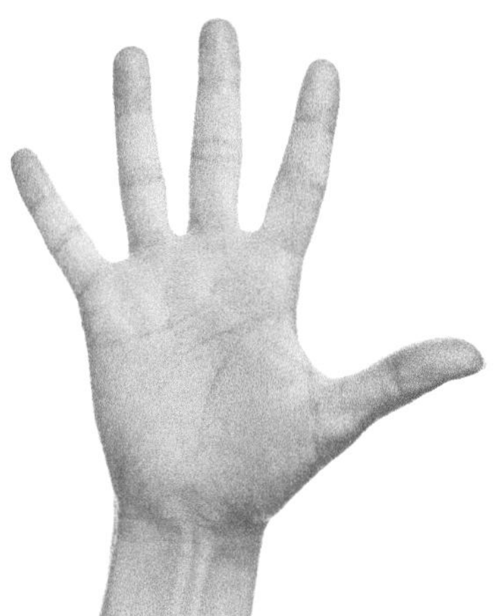

> Emotion is processed 200–5,000 times faster than thought.
>
> —Steven Stosny, *The Powerful Self*[13]

Limbic lava: An emotional response just below the middle prefrontal area can explode into out-of-control activity. Hunger, fatigue, the meaning of an event—almost anything can trigger it. The middle prefrontal cortex is the part of the brain that "calms the reactive lower limbic and brain stem layers—[when it] stops being able to regulate all the energy being stirred up and the coordination and balance of the brain is disrupted…we flip our lids."[14]

It is the prefrontal cortex that keeps the amygdala "contained within the hand." When the brain is regulated and integrated in this way, emotional meltdowns are prevented from occurring.

Brain behavior

How does the ANS play a role in brain behavior?

When the ANS detects danger, it immediately sends a message to the brain stem. The brain stem must assess if it needs to run, fight, or freeze. If the message is that there is safety, then there is no need to respond.

This is where choice, context, and connection come into play immediately. If I have been in this situation before (context), what choices did I use that helped me stay safe and connected? If nothing worked or my responses to the context are hardwired into my brain, I go there immediately without thought. Do I have any connections here that can help me? Do I have any other choices?

When there is an out-of-control response, the first thing that must be done (after safety protocols) is to calm the student. There is no point in having a conversation, because their prefrontal cortex activity is limited at this point.

Ventral
(safe/connected)

My brain is integrated. The prefrontal cortex is regulating the response. My cortex is selecting language. The prefrontal cortex can flex its responses appropriate to the context.

Fight or Flight
SNS mobilized

My amygdala is in charge. My prefrontal cortex is disabled. I will fight and/or run. I will have an "in your face" response. I will not work with you.

Dorsal Vagal

My brain stem is in charge. I have immobilized. I have gone back to survival. I am disengaged.

Strategies

Calming techniques

What are calming techniques?

a. Water—Have the student drink a glass of water. Water helps the body metabolize cortisol, which is produced when someone gets physically upset. When the shoulders relax, the water has been effective in metabolizing the cortisol.

b. Future story—A future story describes what the student wants to do, be, and/or have at the age of 25. In first grade we start by having them wear different hats that represent different occupations. The discussion in the classroom is: "You have a firefighter's helmet! Now, why would you need to know math to be a firefighter?" By fourth grade the future story can be visual. Take a sheet of paper, and have the students put six boxes on the page. In the first box is a picture of their high school diploma. In the second box is how they will continue their education after high school (trade/technical school, military, college, etc.). The third box is what they will do for work. The fourth box is how much money they want to make. The fifth box is a picture of where they will live, and the sixth box is about the kind of vehicle they will drive. Then the students make a plan for getting there, and they identify the obstacles that will get in the way. At the secondary level, there are nine boxes.

Visual future story board

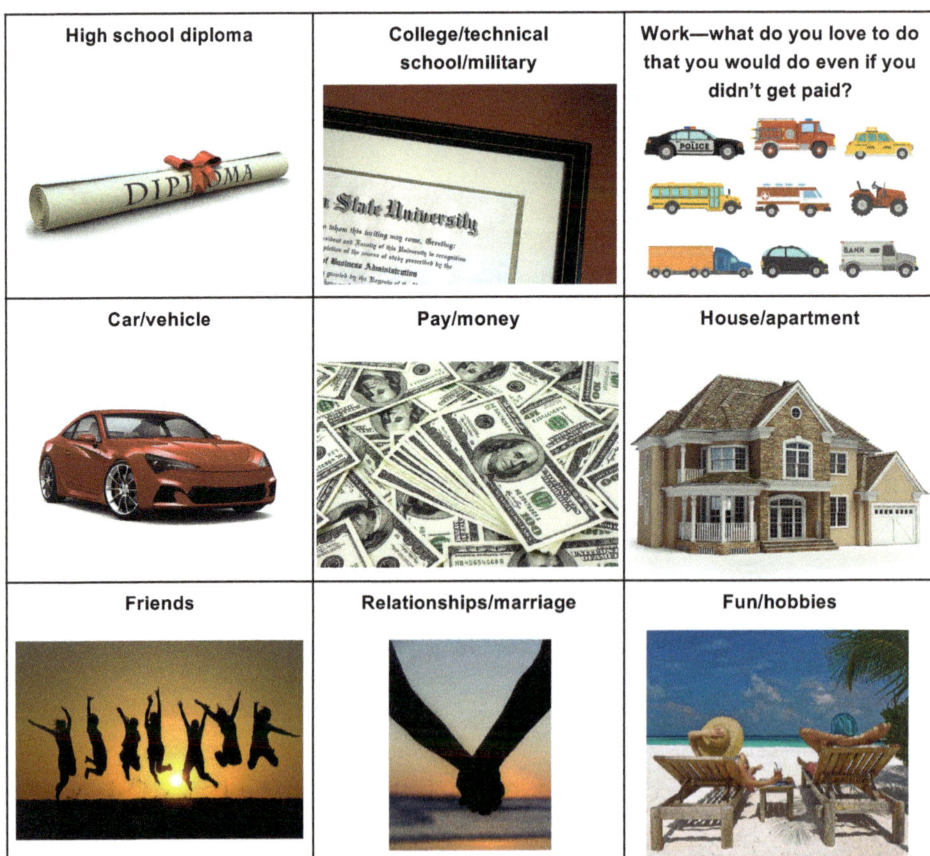

c. Tapping and touch—Books like *Tapping the Healer Within* and *Gorilla Thumps & Bear Hugs* claim that techniques based in traditional Chinese medicine can be used to calm and heal. There's no scientific evidence that these techniques work, but the anecdotal evidence shows that they are very effective with children.[15]

d. More importantly, these techniques do not harm children, so you can feel free to give them a try. Even something as simple as holding a child's hand can be a calming shield against an emotional meltdown. These techniques won't work with every student, but it won't do the students any harm to try.

e. Look up—Simply making the eyes go upward by looking at the ceiling can help calm students who are having an emotional meltdown, especially if they are crying. When eyes are up across the top of the head, the brain is processing visual information. When eyes are moving between the ears, the brain is processing auditory information. When eyes are down, the brain tends to be processing emotional or kinesthetic information. The anecdotal evidence is that looking up makes it more difficult (or even impossible) to access emotions. And it's a momentary distraction that helps students pause and regulate their responses. If you watch students, their shoulders will tend to relax as the intensity of their emotional response lessens. If you ask students to make their eyes go up and look at the ceiling, it is very hard for their brains to process feelings, so typically, students will quit crying and calm down. And, like the tapping approaches described previously, there's no chance it will harm students.

f. Breathing technique—When individuals get upset, they tend to breathe much more shallowly. They tend to breathe from the upper chest. To calm an individual down, have them stand up, inhale deeply from their diaphragm, squeeze their stomach muscles, and hold the deep breath for several seconds before exhaling.

g. Pat your heart and stomach—left hand over heart and rub, right hand over stomach and rub—both at the same time. Your gut has more receptors for serotonin (a calming chemical) than almost any other part of your body, and massage increases serotonin levels.

Understanding the structures of the brain and how they can be integrated and regulated is crucial. So is understanding what it looks like in the classroom when integration and regulation fail—or worse, what it looks like when they were never fully developed in the first place.

The calming techniques listed above can help bring integration and regulation to a brain in crisis. The anecdotal evidence shows they work, and the important thing is they don't harm students, so there is nothing to lose in trying them in your own classroom.

Of course, calming techniques and brain regulation are only part of the story. If the student's inner self is underdeveloped, emotional meltdowns are likely to continue and may even escalate into more intense responses.

What about anxiety?

When people are anxious, they spend time in the dorsal vagal.

Anxiety can come from the prefrontal cortex (What if…?) and is very related to not perceiving that there is safety and belonging. Anxiety can also come from the amygdala; this type of anxiety is often experienced often as a panic attack.

In the book *The Anxious Generation: How the Great Rewiring of Childhood Is Causing an Epidemic of Mental Illness* by Jonathan Haidt, he identifies these four "foundational harms: social deprivation, sleep deprivation, attention fragmentation, and addiction"[16] as culprits in this process. Interestingly, these four also trigger the ANS.

Why do poverty and instability often create more discipline issues?

1. The greater the level of instability (people or resources) in an environment, the more need there is to live in the SNS—run or fight—which disables the prefrontal cortex. The prefrontal cortex controls impulsivity. In a University of California, Berkeley, brain study, they found that the development of the prefrontal cortex in children was significantly less than in children from stable, resourced households.
2. Poverty and instability environments often have a great deal of danger in them. Therefore, the environment hardwires the ANS to be sensitive to danger, to react.
3. If people are in and out of your environment, if your mobility is high and you move a lot, or if there is a lack of adults who are safe, then it is almost impossible to operate at the engagement level of the hierarchy.
4. When running or fighting does not work to stay safe, then a person will go to the dorsal vagal—disengagement—which further reduces the access to safe individuals.

Summary

1. The autonomic nervous system is key in behavioral responses.
2. The majority of discipline referrals occur because the student is functioning in the SNS or the dorsal vagal of the ANS.
3. The greater the level of perceived danger, the greater the opportunity for disengagement or fighting.

4. When the ANS signals a lack of safety, the amygdala reacts and the student goes to the SNS (fighting or running) or to disengagement. Because the amygdala disables the prefrontal cortex in this event, it will take the student about 25 minutes (or more) for their prefrontal cortex to function. Therefore, calming strategies need to be used with the student.

CHAPTER 4

THE IMPACT OF UNSTABLE RESOURCES ON THE AUTONOMIC NERVOUS SYSTEM, HOMELESSNESS, AND SURVIVAL

Unstable resources

What do instability, homelessness, and survival do to the autonomic nervous system? First of all, at a minimum, they force people to act out of the SNS. And if fighting or running does not work, then they often go to the dorsal vagal. The dorsal vagal is the "I give up" stage.

Resources are the tools people use to stay stable. Money is only one of them.

Eleven resources

Rate your own resource base. Where are your strengths? What resources are weaker? How do they stabilize or destabilize your reality?

RESOURCE	Very Stable (3)	Stable (2)	Unstable (1)
Financial Having the money to purchase goods and services.			
Emotional Being able to choose/control emotional responses, particularly to negative situations, without engaging in self-destructive behavior.			
Mental Having the mental abilities and acquired skills (reading, writing, computing) to deal with daily life.			
Language Having the vocabulary, language ability, and negotiation skills to negotiate the environments necessary to build resources.			
Social capital Includes both bonding capital (connections with people similar to yourself) and bridging capital (connections with people different from yourself). Keeps one from being socially isolated.			
Health Any health problems you have are managed and do not interfere with your ability to work and be self-sufficient. You have access to culturally competent healthcare providers.			
Integrity and trust Having the ability to keep your word, honor the laws that govern you, and make decisions based on high ethical standards. It is equally important to be able to trust others to act with integrity.			

RESOURCE	Very Stable (3)	Stable (2)	Unstable (1)
Motivation and persistence The energy and drive to prepare for, plan, and complete projects, jobs, and changes. These are connected to resiliency, the willingness to try, and the courage, stamina, and fortitude to work toward a goal.			
Relationships / role models Having frequent access to adults who are nurturing and caring and who do not engage in destructive behavior. Having friends, family, and backup resources available to access in times of need.			
Knowledge of hidden rules Knowing the unspoken cues and habits of a group.			
Spiritual Believing in divine purpose and that you are part of something larger than yourself.			

If you lack the resource of health, this is responsible for 75% of personal bankruptcies. If you do not have your health, then you cannot work, then you do not have money, then you lose social connections.

Resources are what are used to stabilize our realities. In the book *Scarcity*, the authors identify that scarcity of time or money leads to a drop of 13 IQ points.[17]

What happens with scarcity is that the allostatic load of the brain increases. Basically, there is not enough "bandwidth" to deal with everything that is happening, so your prefrontal cortex is not nearly as effective.

There is a continuum of resources. Resources ebb and flow all of your life. The fewer your resources, the more you live on the left-hand side of the chart. The more your resources, the more you live on the right-hand side of the chart. In the middle is where your resources are stable—you know where you will sleep at night, and you know you have food every day.

Continuum of resources

UNDER-RESOURCED		RESOURCED
Instability/crisis	....	Stability
Isolation	....	Exposure
Dysfunction	....	Functionality
Concrete reality	....	Abstract, representational reality
Casual, oral language	....	Written, formal register
Thought polarization	....	Option seeking
Survival	....	Abundance
No work / intermittent work	....	Work / careers / larger cause
Poverty	....	Wealth
Less educated	....	More educated

Activity

Suppose you make more than minimum wage in many states—$10 an hour—and you are actually lucky enough to get 40 hours a week. That equals $400 a week x 4 weeks in a month is $1,600 a month. There are three people in your household.

Start subtracting from $1,600 by answering these questions:

1. How much will be taken out of your paycheck a month before you get it for FICA, taxes, etc.? Subtract it.
2. What is the least expensive one-bedroom apartment or trailer you can get in your attendance zone with no housing support? Subtract it.
3. What is the least amount of money three people can live on for groceries for a month? Subtract it.
4. What is the least amount you can spend a month on a phone (buying time), utilities, and water? Subtract it.
5. What is the least amount of money you can spend a month on childcare for one child? Subtract it.
6. What is the least amount of money you can spend on a used car and gasoline a month? Subtract it.
7. You are now out of money. What will you do?

Homelessness

CANVA

Could you survive homelessness?

Consider the following to find out:

1. I can go at least 24 hours without food.
2. I know where I can get free food once every day within walking distance.
3. I can wear the same clothes for a week.
4. I can go without a bath/shower for weeks.
5. I know how to protect my feet. Because I walk a lot every day, I also know where I can sit and rest my feet.
6. I know how to protect myself from dangerous people or have someone who will protect me.
7. When the weather is bad, I know a few places that I can go to be protected from the weather.
8. I have people who allow me to "couch surf."
9. I can keep track of my identity (ID) documents, even though I move frequently.
10. I know where I can charge my cell phone and from which buildings (outside or inside) I can access their Internet.
11. I know which libraries will let me in and how long I can stay.
12. I know how to get socks without money.

13. If I am female, I know how to get sanitary supplies.
14. I keep a few first aid supplies on me if I can get them.
15. If I have a dog, I know how to get food for my dog.
16. I know who will buy my medicine if I need to sell it for food.
17. I know where I can sell my blood plasma.
18. I know how to live in my car.
19. I sleep with things on me so that they do not get stolen at the shelter.

To be homeless is to be at one of the highest levels of instability.

How does the McKinney–Vento Act define homelessness?

The McKinney–Vento Act defines homeless children and youths as "individuals who lack a fixed, regular, and adequate nighttime residence." This includes situations such as:

- Staying with friends or relatives due to economic hardship
- Living in hotels, motels, trailer parks, or camping grounds without a choice
- Staying in emergency or transitional shelters
- Living in public spaces such as parks or abandoned buildings
- Migratory students[18]

Being homeless impacts the future story of an individual significantly. If you are homeless as a child, you are much more likely to be homeless during adulthood.

Activity: What does mobility do to your resources?

You are a 10-year-old. Your mother wakes you up in the middle of the night and says, "We are moving. Here is a garbage bag. You have 15 minutes to put in the bag what you want to take. We are not coming back here." Her sister, your aunt, will pick you up in her car. There are five of you: your mother, you, and three siblings. What will you put in your bag?

Students who have experienced homelessness face significantly reduced graduation rates

Homelessness forces a high level of mobility, making it very difficult to maintain learning, keep social connections, have good health, and plan.

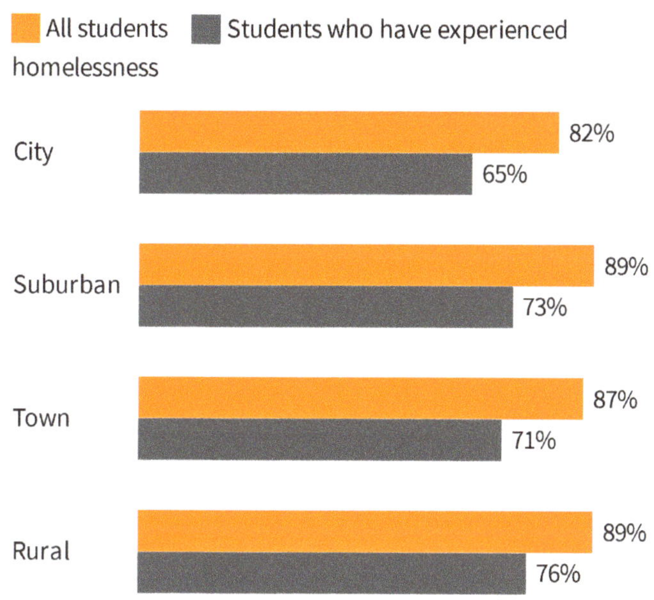

Children experiencing homelessness are:

- nine times more likely to repeat a grade,
- three times more likely to be placed in special education,
- and four times more likely to drop out of school entirely.

How many children are homeless in the United States?

- One in every 30 American children goes to sleep without a home of his or her own each year.
- Approximately 2.5 million children are homeless annually in the United States.
- On any given day, there are approximately 443,000 children in foster care in the United States.[19]

Here are some facts you should know about family and child homelessness:

- 29% of homeless families are headed by a working adult, usually the mother.
- More than half of homeless mothers do not have a high school diploma.
- Approximately 63% of homeless women have been victims of domestic violence.
- Homeless children are more likely to suffer from hunger and poor physical and emotional health.
- Homeless children are less likely to attend school and more likely to fall behind in class.
- While the number of homeless children in the United States is estimated at 1.6 million, many estimates suggest the number could be far higher, as homelessness statistics are often underreported at the city, county, and state levels.

Meet Rene

"I was so hungry all of the time and I remember my mommy waking me up early on Saturday mornings so we could have breakfast from a church who served it under the bridge with other homeless people. Sometimes we got to share a bed and other times we slept with people in a big room at the homeless shelter. It was always scary. I wore the same clothes every day because mommy said we couldn't carry too much while we walked around looking for food and a place to sleep. The shelters were so cold and their blankets were very thin, but it was way better than the nights outside. I cried when my mommy told me that we finally had a home to live in and that I would never be cold and hungry again."[20]

- Homeless children experience four times as many respiratory infections, twice as many ear infections, and are four times more likely to have asthma.
- By the age of 12, 83% of homeless children have experienced violence.
- Homeless children have three times the rate of emotional and behavioral problems.
- The longer children stay on the street, the farther behind they fall in school.
- 42% of children in homeless families are under age six.

Strategies to stabilize resources for students who are in instability and homelessness

At the district or campus level

1. Identify whether or not the child can qualify for a 504 plan, which will provide extra services to the student. Many homeless students have anxiety (which qualifies them for a 504 plan), given the constant instability of resources, people, and context.
2. Get four or five cell phone numbers from different people connected to the student so there is a way to maintain contact. Often when you are homeless, you buy cell phones from Walmart that have minutes but not a plan. Things get lost because of the constant movement, so the more contact points you have, the greater the chances of providing support to the student.
3. Give an educational assessment to determine at what academic level the student is performing to determine the necessary tutoring supports that might be needed.
4. Determine what access the student has to the Internet, Wi-Fi, and digital devices. Identify sources close to where they are currently staying (library, coffee shop, etc.) where they might have access.
5. Provide a place on each campus where legal paperwork can be done on a computer with an Internet connection. Legal paperwork, applications, forms, identification, etc., are very difficult to do on a phone and very difficult to do if you do not know formal register.
6. Join Bright Futures (www.brightfutures.org). For a one-time fee of $3,000, you can use their model to connect to churches via social media (students' identities are protected) and get specific resources for a student. (For example, we need one size 8 pair of athletic shoes.)

7. Stabilize the parent by providing Getting Ahead classes. The return on investment is significant to the individual and the community. See www.ahaprocess.com for more information.
8. Assign a "buddy," an ambassador, to the new student. They make sure that during the first week of school, the student does not eat lunch alone or play alone at recess (elementary). On the first day the student is there, they take them to each of their classes (secondary) so they know where they are going.
9. Provide a place the student can keep paperwork/books/tablets at school. Homelessness is chaotic, and it is difficult to find paperwork, etc.
10. Assign an adult who does a check-in with the student on a regular basis.
11. Establish a texting protocol with the parent or guardian. Ask them if they will just use the word "OK" if the child is okay that day.
12. Make certain that tutoring is accessible to the student—time frames, location, Internet, etc.
13. Provide structure, a consistent routine, and clear expectations. It will reduce the allostatic load for the student.
14. Identify a small group or one person with whom the student can develop a connection. Males tend to bond over shared activities. Females tend to bond over shared conversations.
15. Determine the level of safety the student has outside of school. Is there violence, abuse, etc., from which the student needs to be shielded? (It should be noted that the number one reason for women with children being homeless is domestic violence.)

In the classroom

Remember: Sleeping in homeless shelters is difficult. There is always someone crying, snoring, dreaming, awake, talking, arguing. Blankets are thin or limited. If they fall asleep in class, let them sleep. If they lose their work, allow it. If they don't return materials, forget it.

As a teacher, you cannot possibly meet all the needs of your homeless students. Accept that. But if you are that one person who greets them each morning, who helps them co-regulate for that day, you have made a tremendous difference for that student.

You may be the safest part of their day.

Frustrations for students who are homeless
Frustrations for teachers who teach students who are homeless

For students	For teachers
Ashamed of where they live (especially if at a shelter).	Students may have lived in many places, attending different schools with different teaching methods. No school records.
Teased by other students about homelessness, hygiene, and inabilities. Misunderstood by parents.	Need to assess educational needs without prior records.
Difficulty adjusting to new school, magnified by situation.	Need to do a quick assessment of student, as formal measures are too time-consuming.
No place to do homework (or quiet place for themselves).	Knowledge that the student may move soon.
Developmental delay augments feelings of failure.	Other students may react negatively.
	Students may have difficulty trusting. Inability to contact parents in an emergency. Parents often emotionally unavailable. Homework completion can be difficult.

Suggestions for teachers helping students who are homeless

- Make the child feel welcome.
- Make the new student a file that includes things to send home to parents (e.g., school rules, classroom rules, lunchroom rules, class schedule, and a list of special classes).
- Provide well-defined transition procedures from one activity to another.
- Plan ahead whenever possible, and inform students ahead of time about substitute teachers and changes in activities. This will foster a sense of safety and security.

- Coordinate any educational plan with the school counselor. Expect and unobtrusively monitor regressions.
- Offer encouragement and understanding, and recognize the child's talents and accomplishments. Give students the opportunity to see some of their experiences as positive (e.g., places they have traveled).
- Allow personal possessions, and keep in mind that any possession may be the child's only one. Give choices when appropriate to counter the loss of control experienced in their lives.
- Don't penalize students who are homeless for being late before finding out if they have reliable transportation and an alarm clock.
- Assign projects that can be broken into small components to ensure students have at least some success. The experience of mastery is critical to their self-image.
- Maintain the child's privacy, and discuss homework situations away from other classmates.
- Avoid assignments that require TV, Internet, devices, streaming (students living in shelters may not be able to make the choices, may not have access, etc.).
- Show sensitivity when asking children to bring food, photographs, favorite toys, or other items from home. Children who are homeless are often embarrassed to admit that they do not have these things.
- Avoid taking away recess/gym class as a disciplinary consequence. (This may be the only time students who are homeless have space to run.) Children are often without an adequate play area at shelters or in the streets.
- Don't assume younger students know how to play. They may have to be taught how to do so.
- Help the child participate in field trips, school activities, and class projects through understanding her/his living environment and access to resources. Arrange school picture fees so children who are homeless may have pictures, too.
- Ensure that children in homeless situations have easy access to assistance in case of personal difficulties (e.g., counselors). Allow students to express fears and frustrations, and allow opportunities to do so in other ways in addition to verbalizing (e.g., drawing). Help children find positive outlets for anger.

- Help children take an active role in their life. A sense of empowerment is critical to overcoming helplessness. (For example, make the child a helper in class, have the child tutor a younger child, promote activities they are good at.)
- Understand that the parents are often overwhelmed and are operating at the dorsal vagal level.
- Know that students are often the caretakers for the adults. They will be offended when treated as children.

Summary

1. There are 11 resources that can help to stabilize your context (environment).
2. The more unstable the resources become, the more the person will function in the SNS or the dorsal vagal.
3. The closer an individual gets to survival, the less ability there is to plan because resources are so unpredictable.
4. Homelessness and its disruptive nature can limit academic learning.

CHAPTER 5

THE ROLE OF NEGOTIATING CONTEXT (ENVIRONMENT):

How You Spend Your Time Determines What You Know, Who You Know, and the Rules for Survival

One of the ways that we are all alike in the world is that we have 24 hours each day. There is a simple rule: How you spend your time determines to a large extent who and what you know. I saw a documentary on a homeless 17-year-old boy in Los Angeles. They asked him how he spends his time. He said he spends seven to eight hours a day finding food. If that is what you spend your time doing, then there is a lot of information you do not have time to learn because you are in survival.

In order to negotiate their environment, individuals use who and what they know, their resources, and the demands of the environment to stabilize and stay alive.

Please note: In the following mental models, most people have a foot in two worlds, and some people have their feet in all three. The issue is how many contexts you are able to negotiate.

What is this cognitive frame?

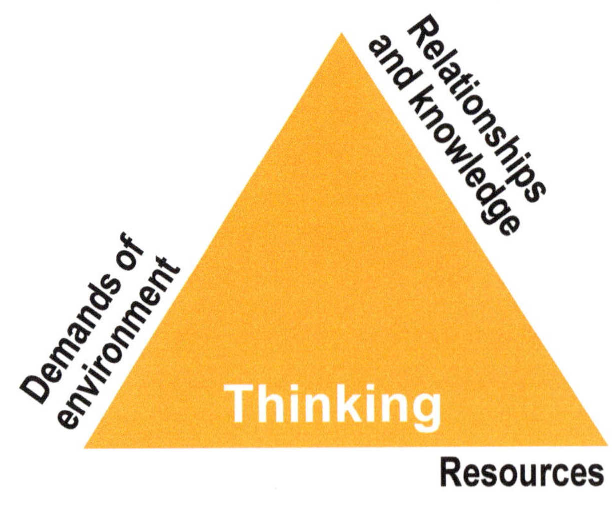

A COGNITIVE MODEL

Below is a set of mental models—what you spend your time on when resources are unstable (poverty), when resources are stable, and when there is an excess of resources (wealth).

This first chart is a mental model of instability—when resources are thin or nonexistent. Relationships are the stabilizer in this context. The institutions that you tend to use are schools, social services, police, and religious/nonprofit institutions. The businesses that you tend to use are pawnshops, rent-to-own, check-cashing services, laundromats, corner stores, fast food, used car lots, temp services, and dollar stores. Many homeless individuals live in this context. To survive in this world, you have to have someone who can physically protect you if you cannot do it for yourself.

Mental model of poverty / instability

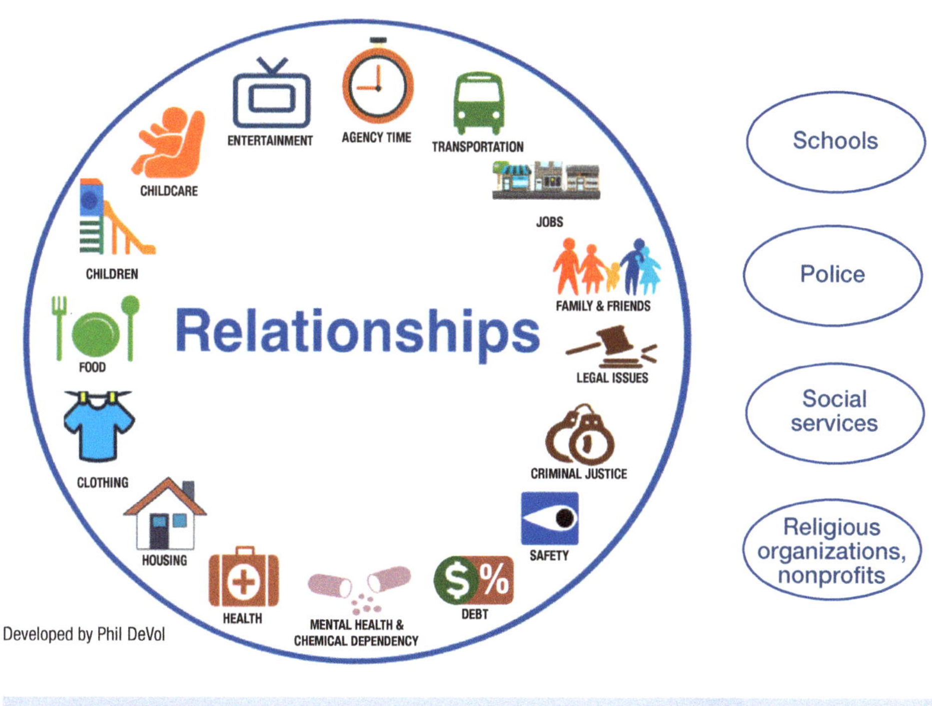

Developed by Phil DeVol

Businesses

Pawnshops	Laundromats	Used car lots
Liquor stores	Fast food	Dollar stores
Corner stores	Check cashing	
Rent-to-own	Temp services	

This next chart is what is more characteristic of a context where resources are more stable and predictable. The driving force for stability is achievement, and typically, this group spends their time working, getting more education, and acquiring assets (like a mortgage). The institutions and activities that they interface with are universities, medical providers, sports and fitness, religious organizations, civic groups, and professional and career-related organizations. The businesses that they tend to frequent include shopping malls, bookstores, banks, fitness centers, vet clinics, office complexes, coffee shops, restaurants and bars, golf courses, new car lots, etc. In this world, you protect yourself with security systems.

Mental model of middle class / stability

Developed by Phil DeVol

Businesses

Shopping/strip malls	Fitness centers	Coffee shops
Bookstores	Veterinary clinics	Restaurants/bars
Banks	Office complexes	Golf courses

When your resources are excessive, as is shown in the next chart, then you have a different problem in your context. You cannot manage all of your resources yourself, so you hire people to help you. That impacts your personal safety—people can rob or kidnap you. So in this context, time is more important than money. You can always make more money, but you cannot make more time. Time becomes one of your most valuable resources. This is the world of social, financial, and political connections that stabilize your resource base.

The institutions and services that are accessed in this mental model include spas, private clubs, golf courses, plastic surgery, concierge services, security services, personal shoppers, media management firms, upscale travel, flight-

Mental model of wealth

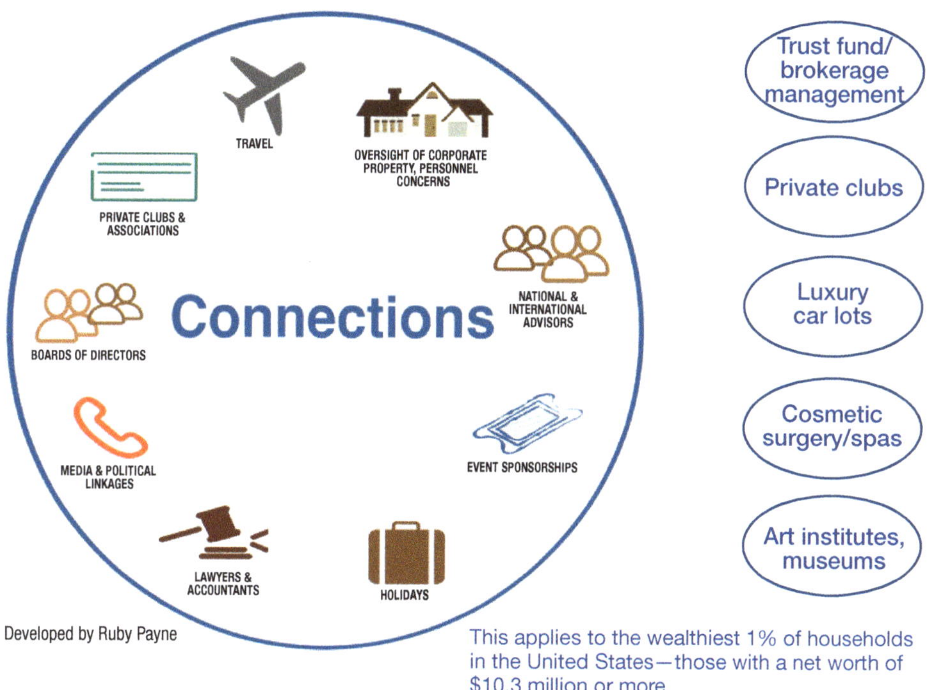

Developed by Ruby Payne

This applies to the wealthiest 1% of households in the United States—those with a net worth of $10.3 million or more.

Businesses

Spas	Luxury car lots	Party planners
Private clubs	Personal shoppers	Upscale hotels
Golf courses	Boutique shopping areas	Private airports with charter and corporate jets
Plastic surgery	Private schools	Upscale travel offices
Concierge services	Personal security	Fine wine and alcohol
Pet spas	Florists	

based operations, charter air services, party planners, architectural firms, interior decorating firms, facilities management firms, etc. The businesses that are accessed include trust fund / brokerage management firms, foundation boards, management firms of all kinds, international law firms, and the like.

These tend to be the driving forces behind how you spend time and money.

Hidden rules about time and money

INSTABILITY	STABILITY	WEALTH
Survival	Work	Political connections
Relationships	Achievement	Financial connections
Entertainment	Material security	Social connections

The reason for explaining these circles is simple: If you are homeless or in survival, you will use the rules and understandings of the first circle of instability. Yet schools operate out of the second circle of stability. Their knowledge bases, behaviors, and understandings are different. However, we expect students who are homeless or have instability to automatically know how to negotiate a different context. This disconnect is frustrating to those individuals and is frustrating to staff.

Each of these environments has understandings that are unspoken—hidden rules, if you will. These knowledge bases and understandings show up in many ways: rules for acceptable behavior, understandings about how you negotiate an environment (context), and how you handle feelings. There are often hidden rules about how to deal with a situation.

For example, in instability (survival circle), you are respected if you are "tough and strong." Showing emotion (crying) is considered a form of weakness and is not respected. Yet, if you get drunk, stoned, or high, that is acceptable because you "toughed it out." Admitting that you have anxiety would not be respected, but an addiction would be understood, as would a response of violence.

Counseling and therapy are not respected. If you take medications for mental or emotional illness issues, and you get Supplemental Security Income from the government, that money is often referred to as a "crazy check."

Choices when you have limited resources or are homeless are very limited. The idea that you would plan a future is nonexistent. Today is about survival. The connections you have are often for survival. In survival contexts, if you cannot physically fight or have someone to fight for you, your safety is at risk.

In the stable circle (middle class norms), it is acceptable to talk about your feelings, go to a therapist, or tell your friends about your issues. It is acceptable to take prescription medicines for anxiety. Connections tend to be for shared activities, sports, and causes.

In the very resourced circle, virtually everyone has a mentor, coach, or therapist. Emotional information is shared with a certified professional, not openly with friends. Discretion is very important. Connections are fostered for political, social, and economic reasons. In this context, the lawyers do the fighting. The weapon of choice is social exclusion. You are just not invited.

Strategies

1. Direct teach the rules of each context so there is less anxiety.
2. In the appendix is a three-part quiz adapted from Chapter Three in *A Framework for Understanding Poverty* about hidden rules. Understand that there will be "acceptable ways" to handle the ANS based upon your context. It will help you understand some of the realities.
3. If you are homeless or grew up in survival, there will be many knowledge bases you do not have. It does not mean that you are not intelligent. It just means you did not have the opportunity to learn those things in your context. Direct teach the knowledge bases that you need for survival in school.

Summary

1. There is a relationship between how you spend your time and who and what you know.
2. Each context (circle) offers different choices, understandings, and rules about how to survive.
3. For students who are homeless or in unstable contexts, schooling assumes they will be able to function well in a different context without instruction.

CHAPTER 6

DISENGAGEMENT FROM CONTEXT: THE ABSTRACT REALITIES OF SCHOOL

This chapter outlines some of the demands in the context of schooling that are difficult to negotiate and that create disengagement and withdrawal.

Abstract representational systems

Abstract representational systems, which are used often in education settings, remove students from concrete, sensory realities and often seem irrelevant to survival.

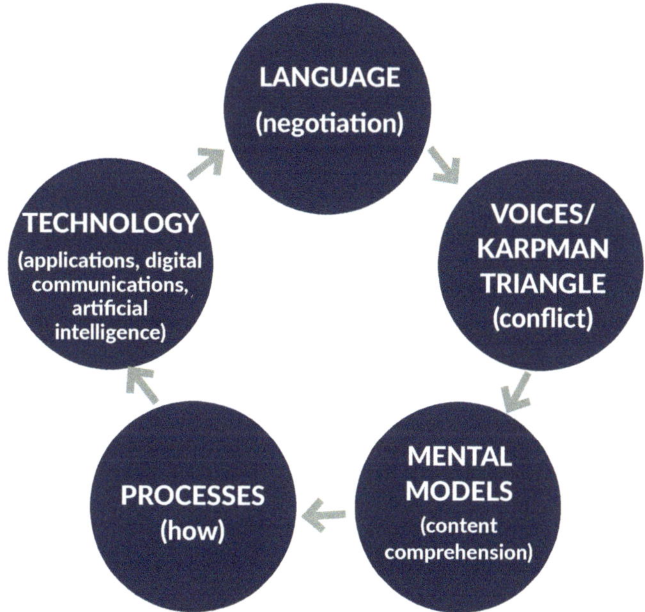

Most of the approaches to teaching and learning address issues that focus on teaching. This chapter is focusing on the learning part. In other words, what must a student do inside their head to learn and then be able to use the information?

In order to survive in school, a learner must be able to negotiate the abstract representational world, which is the paper world, or the world as represented on a computer screen. This takes a different skill set because of the requirement that sensory information be represented on paper. For example, an apple in three dimensions does not look like a two-dimensional drawing of an apple. The drawing only represents the apple on paper. Words represent a feeling, but they are not the feeling. A photo represents a person, but it is not the person. Numbers represent an amount, but they are not the actual item being counted.

Vocabulary becomes the tool with which the mind categorizes information (like and different), sorts the information, assigns the information to a pattern or group, and then communicates shared meaning. One of the misunderstandings of constructivism was that as long as students made meaning inside their heads, they were okay. But meaning has value only to the extent that it can be shared and communicated. This requires a collective understanding of what a word means. Vocabulary is the key tool for thinking.

What is the paper world?

The paper world is how information and understandings are conveyed in formal schooling. Words, symbols, etc., are used to convey the meaning. Paper doesn't have nonverbals, emotions, or human interaction. Paper depends on a shared understanding of vocabulary in order to communicate. If you grew up in a household where there were very few books, calendars, clocks, etc., the concept of information on paper is difficult. It has to be learned.

Continuum of paper documents

As your resources grow and become more complex, the amount of paper documents in a household indicates to some extent your familiarity and comfort with the paper world.

birth certificates
immunization records
driver's licenses
rental agreements
money orders
paycheck stubs / bills

wills
magazines/newspapers
payment records
credit card and bank statements
mortgage papers
calendars
planners
to-do lists
tax returns
books
coupons
passports

corporate financial statements
prenuptial agreements
stock certificates / personal investments
provenance
property deeds
charity events / invitations
board of directors minutes / records
club memberships
trusts

The language you have works for the context you know but not necessarily for the contexts you do not know. The paper world tends to be representational—numbers represent the things, but they are not the things.

One of the *huge* issues when you are homeless is negotiating all of the legal documents and keeping track of them. These include identification documents (driver's license, Social Security number, addresses, immunization records, birth certificate, etc.). Addresses are such an issue, especially if you move a lot. I know of a church who allowed homeless individuals to use their address for mail, for job applications, etc.

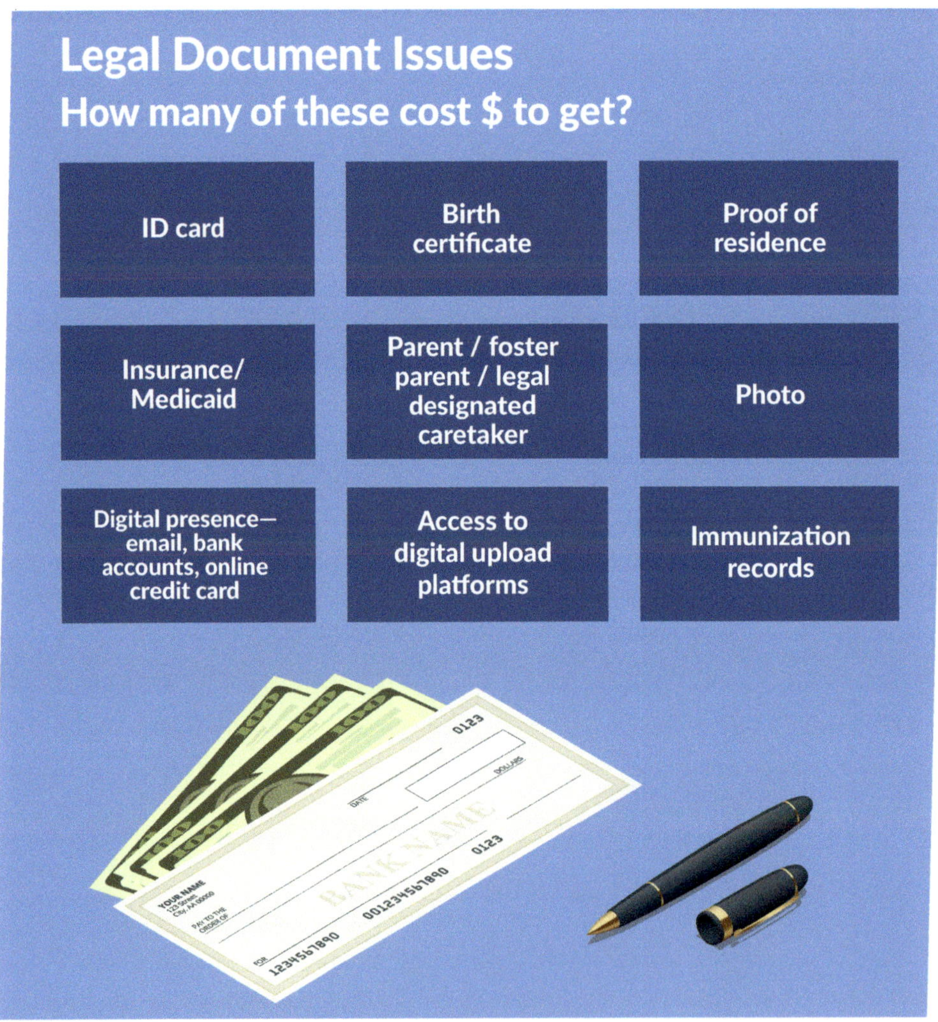

One of the most difficult contexts to negotiate if you come from survival, homelessness, or instability is the abstract representational systems of school, work, business, and legalities. Abstract, decontextualized, representational symbols and ideas are on paper to represent a tangible, sensory reality. Here are some examples:

Abstract item	Represents
Grades	"Ticket" to get into college, a better job, more money
House deed	Physical property
Address	Physical location
Social Security number	Person (a way to keep track of people on paper)
Daily to-do list	Tasks to be accomplished that day
Clock or calendar	Abstract time
State assessment	Knowledge base and personal vocabulary; a representation of shared understandings for communication
Homework	Ability to complete a task in a given time frame in order to establish understandings
Insurance papers	An external support system that provides money, assistance, and expertise for unusual circumstances, health, etc.
Driver's license	The right to physically operate a vehicle
TV guide	Shows or programs
Photograph	The person (a photo doesn't breathe; it's a two-dimensional representation of the person)
Letters in alphabet	Symbols that represent physical sounds that together make up words
Numbers	Symbols that represent quantity
Musical notations	Symbols that represent sounds and timing
Road map	Objects, roads, etc., in physical space
Sonogram	A three-dimensional representation of an object
MRI (magnetic resonance imaging)	A three-dimensional representation of a body, body part, etc. (it isn't the body, but it represents the body)
Trust document	A legal entity (has its own Social Security number) that pays taxes, owns property, and identifies how assets will be held and distributed over time
Student handbook	Paper version of the appropriate behaviors that are to be used
Teacher contract	A legal document that establishes expectations for teachers' compensation, benefits, terms of employment, etc.
Menu	The food choices in a restaurant (it isn't the food itself)

Language

CANVA

At the base of the abstract representational world is language. Words, numbers, drawings, maps, etc., are all necessary to negotiate your context. And there are different "levels" or registers of language that can be used depending on the context.

Registers of language

REGISTER	EXPLANATION
FROZEN	Language that is always the same. For example: Lord's Prayer, wedding vows, etc.
FORMAL	The standard sentence syntax and word choice of work and school. Has complete sentences and specific word choice.
CONSULTATIVE	Formal register when used in conversation. Discourse pattern not quite as direct as formal register.
CASUAL	Language between friends, characterized by a 400- to 800-word vocabulary. Word choice general and not specific. Conversation dependent upon nonverbal assists. Sentence syntax often incomplete.
INTIMATE	Language between lovers or twins. Language of sexual harassment.

Adapted from the work of Martin Joos

Frozen register includes words that are always the same. Word choice conveys an exact understanding, as in medicine, law, etc. Formal register is what we use at work and school. It is in writing, with specific word choice. All the testing and textbooks are in formal register. Consultative is the spoken version of formal register and has a lot of casual register in it. Casual register is language between friends and has about half of the words that formal register does. It often uses emojis and nonverbals to convey meaning. Intimate is language between lovers or twins. It is a private language that only those individuals understand.

As you can see in the next chart, researchers put tape recorders in homes by economic class to see how much language a child heard in a three-year time period (ages 1–4). This does not include what was heard on television but instead what was heard among people. Basically, the access to language is less when the resources are limited.

Formal register

Research About Language in Children, Ages 1 to 4, in Stable Households by Economic Group			
Number of words exposed to	**Economic group**	**Affirmations (strokes)**	**Prohibitions (discounts)**
13 million words	Welfare	1 for every	2
26 million words	Working class	2 for every	1
45 million words	Professional	6 for every	1

Note. From *Meaningful Differences in the Everyday Experience of Young American Children*, by B. Hart and T. R. Risley, 1995.

Links to updated research:

http://news.stanford.edu/news/2013/september/toddler-language-gap-091213.html

http://www.ncbi.nlm.nih.gov/pmc/articles/PMC3659033/

http://literacy.rice.edu/thirty-million-word-gap (This is a follow-up study on Hart and Risley.)

All abstract words are in formal register—the language of school and work. What is being used more and more in survival environments is casual register in text messages, along with emojis.

To survive in school, you have to be able to plan, use formal register, and handle paperwork/computer abstract representational systems.

Digital communication

In your handout, translate the redacted text message into formal register in one paragraph. Why can texting create issues in communication?

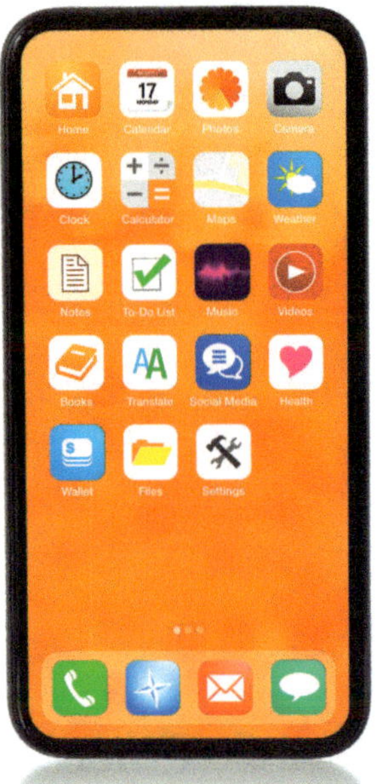

Below is a redacted message via text about K (an adult currently in jail) who is about to be homeless. A relative has died, and he no longer has a place to stay.

If you need to talk to K. 'With your permission' I can give him your number. Of course it's collect @ .14 a min.

When he calls you hv to put your CC number in the recorded msg… he will charge your card…then he can talk to you.

Each time he calls they will verify your exp date / Zip Code. So no one will have your info to charge calls on you.

Let me know.

Just gave K your number. Call me when you hv a moment to explain to you how the call is placed. You hv to give a CC to talk to him… (can be for just 1 call)…make sure to press the right button to do this!

She sd she had a life policy

I remember when you ask me if I wanted you to hv all the stuff in the house removed & take out of my her hous…I said, "No" bc I'm sure we would like to have some of the furniture that was still in good shape.

So I told you I would start the following week. I took some of her clothing 80% I paid for…but others took all they wanted as well.

I also took a Chester drawer & 2 night stand & patio

1 lrg screen TV & 1 small…all of which I paid for. Did I consult anybody…no I did not. Can not communicate with those two siblings. Too much anger

They took the car. All her jewelry diamonds/ pearls, bags / box of clothing… ALL the food in all refrig-erators & freezer, etc

They paid for "absolutely nothing" in her house.

They just want to receive/take. Contributed absolutely nothing.

Some of what I took was to share with K or else he would hv nothing. Since he's gone…when he returns there would be nothing for him… the youngest thinks everything belong to him…well it does not.

You make the call!

K may have extra keys to her car…if he does. He will take the car from the brother's house…that will definitely be a fight btw the two of them.

Both feels entitled !

Both are angry with hot tempers.

my sister's husband will be picking K up tonight around midnight. K has already said he's going back to her house.

K said he will help with cleaning the house & the outside…but with the intent…he thinks staying there. I'm not sure what you told home.

It's heavy trash on Saturday for the area…I will do my best to get rid of as much as I can…hopefully with some family help.

But I keep my distance from you know who…drama drama drama

Thank you for all you've done…according to her will & wish. I know it was a challenge but you proved to be a faithful steward & friend to her

I can not thank you enough! See & talk to you soon.

This is an answer to prayer. I shut down my business to show love…

but that's love & sacrifice…I just prayed to the Lord…he sees all. He is faithful & he is our rewarder!

But I had asked in advance…P told me he would…but did not. Will you pls pls pls ask him.

It's a keepsake. This is where she spent most of her time with us ! Pls pls pls

It's hard for me to think that she did not hv life insurance…it's doesn't matter to me who she made as beneficiaries.

I certainly didn't think it would be me. But I asked her about it 3 times. She sd…"you will find it when it's time". So I assume there was one.

By that stmt I assumed she did not want me to know anything about it so I left it along. Someday I'll get to reward you for your love & labor

Activity

1. Translate this text message into formal register.
2. If this is the way information is given in your household, why would school be difficult?

Strategies

Strategy to improve formal register: To use this strategy, each student receives these four documents. Twice a week, in the area of content you are teaching, identify two words that the student figures out the meaning of by using prefixes, root words, and suffixes. For example, in transportation, *trans* means across, *port* means to carry, and *-ation* means the process of doing that. Students will say that makes no sense. And we tell them that they have to move the words around—transportation is the process of carrying things across.

This is a wonderful strategy for helping students do well on state assessments and the SAT and ACT.

Most commonly used prefixes

Prefix: a word part that can be added to the beginning of a root or base word that changes the meaning of a root or base word.

anti = against	auto = self	bi = two
circum = around	co, con, com = with	contra = against
de = opposite	dis = reverse/opposite	e, ex = out
en, em = cause to	in, im, il, ir = not	inter = between
macro = large	micro = small	mid = middle
mis = wrongly	mono = one	non = not
poly = many	post = after	pre = before
re = back/again	semi = partly	sub = under
super = above	syn = same time	trans = across
tri = three	un = not	uni = one

Source: © Educational Epiphany. Reprinted with permission. www.educationalepiphany.com, 2012.

Most commonly used root words

Root: a word part to which affixes (prefixes and suffixes) may be added to create related words.

audi = hear	auto = self	bene = good
bio = life	chrono = time	cred = believe
dict = say	duc = lead	fid = truth, faith
flex = bend	gen = give birth	geo = earth
graph = write	greg = group	jur, jus = law
log = thought	luc = light	man = hand
mand = order	mis, mit = send	omni = all
path = feel	phil = love	phon = sound
photo = light	port = carry	scrib = write
sens, sent = feel	spec, spect, spic = look	tele = far off
terr = earth	vac = empty	vid, vis = see

Source: © Educational Epiphany. Reprinted with permission. www.educationalepiphany.com, 2012.

Most commonly used suffixes

Suffix: a word part added to the end of a root or base word that changes the meaning of a root or base word.

able, ible = can be done	acy = state or quality of	al = act or process of
al, ial = pertaining to	ate = become	dom = place or state of
ed = past tense	el, er, or = one who	er = comparative
en = become	ess = female	ful, ous = full of
ic, ical = pertaining to	ify, fy = make or become	ing = present participle
ion, tion, ation, = act, process	ish = somewhat like or near	ism = characteristic of
ist = one who	ity, ty = quality of	ize, ise = make or become
less = without	ly = characteristic of	ment = act of, result of
ness = state of	ology = study, science	s, es = more than one, plural
ship = position held	ward = in the direction of	y = having the quality of

Source: © Educational Epiphany. Reprinted with permission. www.educationalepiphany.com, 2012.

Understanding and analysis across genres

Determine the meaning of grade level technical academic English words in multiple content areas (science, math, social studies, the arts) derived from Latin, Greek, or other linguistic roots and affixes.

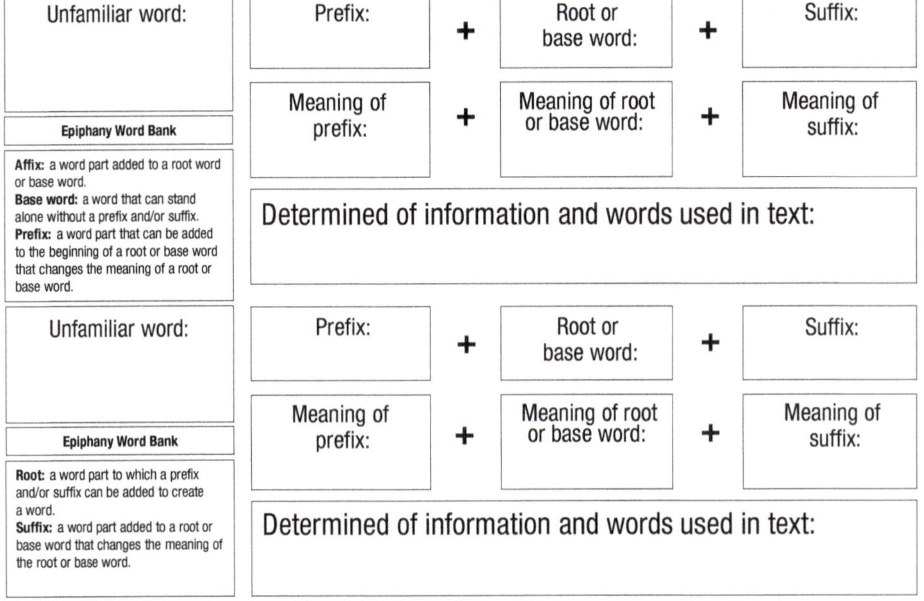

Unfamiliar word:

Prefix: + Root or base word: + Suffix:

Meaning of prefix: + Meaning of root or base word: + Meaning of suffix:

Epiphany Word Bank

Affix: a word part added to a root word or base word.
Base word: a word that can stand alone without a prefix and/or suffix.
Prefix: a word part that can be added to the beginning of a root or base word that changes the meaning of a root or base word.

Determined of information and words used in text:

Unfamiliar word:

Prefix: + Root or base word: + Suffix:

Meaning of prefix: + Meaning of root or base word: + Meaning of suffix:

Epiphany Word Bank

Root: a word part to which a prefix and/or suffix can be added to create a word.
Suffix: a word part added to a root or base word that changes the meaning of the root or base word.

Determined of information and words used in text:

Source: © Educational Epiphany. Reprinted with permission. www.educationalepiphany.com, 2012.

Negotiating choice, context, and connection with language

One of the most interesting aspects of the hierarchy is the fact that it requires physical movement to go from dorsal vagal to the SNS. You can participate in the SNS in casual register. To negotiate the ventral vagal requires at least consultative register (spoken version of formal register) because safe social connections require negotiation. Language is used to seek understanding, come to agreements about how to work together, and do business together.

In the conflict resolution research, you have to go from the personal (casual register) to the issue level to negotiate conflicts. I once heard a husband and wife argue about whom the cat loved the most. They were really arguing about who was most lovable, but they argued about it at a personal level. When you only have casual register, it is very difficult to resolve conflicts.

Voices / Karpman triangle: The abstract world of negotiating conflict

As you negotiate conflict safely, it makes it easier to have social connections. The voice you choose to negotiate with often determines the outcome. When a person moves out of social connection (ventral vagal), they will attempt to negotiate the connection so they can stay there in safety.

ANS hierarchy

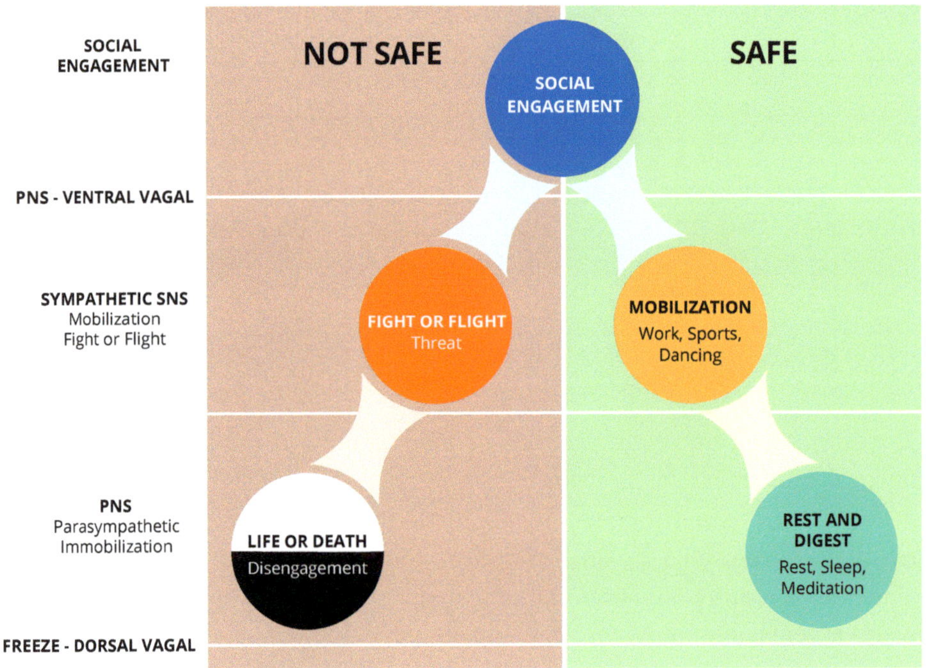

Adapted from the work of Matthew Tobias

Voices indicate your prosody, your voice tone, all of which impact the social engagement system. When you are in the parent voice, it is a telling voice. The adult voice is an asking voice, and the child voice (in conflict) is a whining voice.

The parent voice puts individuals on the defensive almost immediately: "I told you." There is also a firm parent voice: "I need you to do this." The adult voice asks questions in order to understand. The child voice basically whines. If you grew up in a context where you were your own parent or the parenting was very harsh, the research is that you have only two of the three voices: the child voice and the parent voice. It is very difficult to resolve a conflict with only those two voices. The adult voice is what best resolves conflicts.

Voices

Parent (telling)	Child (whining)	Adult (asking)
• You shouldn't do that. • It's wrong to... • That's stupid, immature. • You are good, bad, worthless, beautiful.	• Quit picking on me! • You don't love me! • I hate you! • You're ugly. • It's your fault. • You made me do it.	• I need... • What's your plan? • What are your choices? • If you did know, what would you say?

Adapted from the work of Eric Berne

Negotiation is further impacted by staying out of the Karpman triangle.

Karpman triangle

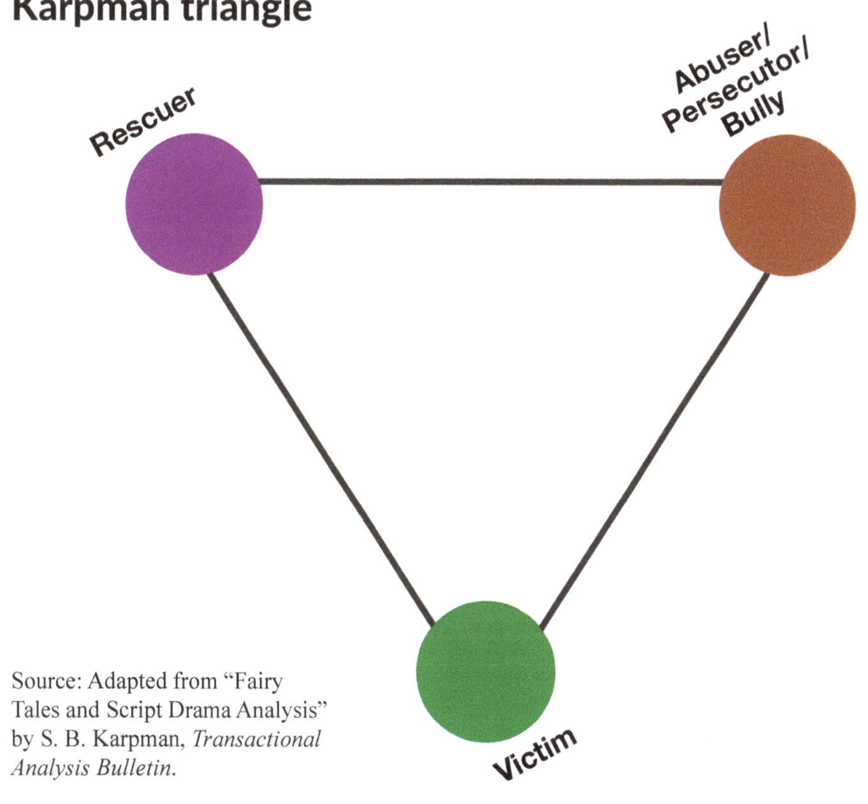

Source: Adapted from "Fairy Tales and Script Drama Analysis" by S. B. Karpman, *Transactional Analysis Bulletin.*

The Karpman triangle often results from using only the parent and child voice. The rules of the Karpman triangle are the following: If you get in the triangle with someone, you will end of taking on all three roles and you will never solve the problem. To stay out of the triangle, you ask fact-based procedural questions. Almost always the victim is in the child voice, the bully is in the parent voice, and the rescuer—unless they ask fact-based procedural questions—will get hijacked by the bully or the victim.

Using procedural, fact-based questions

What does "procedural, fact-based questions" mean?

Educators like to ask motivational questions. Why? What were you thinking? Etc.

Better data can be obtained when you ask procedural questions. Think of your hand. On the palm of your hand, write the word specifically. On your thumb, write the word How? On your other fingers, write these words: What? Where? When? Which one? or Who? Below is an example.

When I was a principal and a parent came in to ask about something, the first question I asked was, "Do you want me to listen, or do you want me to do something about this?" If they said, "Do something about this," then I would say, "Okay, but I need to call in your child and ask some questions to solve this problem." (Sometimes they do not want you to talk to the child, in which case it is not possible to solve the problem because everything becomes hearsay.)

While waiting on the student, I would say to the parent, "Specifically, what did your child tell you about this?" Do you know specifically where this happened? Do you know specifically who was involved with your child in this situation? Do you know when this happened? (It has been my experience that most parents come in angry with very few specifics. The problem can only be solved with facts.)

Then I would ask the child the same questions. Specifically, what happened first? Then what happened? What did you say or do? What did the other person say or do? Where were you when this happened? Has this same thing happened before?

Basically, you just keep asking procedural questions until you know what actually happened—not the interpretation or current understandings, but what actually happened. Then you can get at feelings, solutions, etc.

Generic mental models

Mental models are how the mind holds abstract information, i.e., information that has little or no sensory representation.

Each of us carries much abstract information around in our head every day. How do we do this? We carry it in mental models.

Just as a computer has a file manager to represent the structure of the software content, so does the human mind.

To be successful in school or work, one must have generic mental models. They are:

- Space
- Time
- Part to whole

These mental models are fundamental to all tasks.

Space

Space becomes important because your body operates in space. The mind must have a way to keep track of your body. One way is to touch everything. Another way is to assign a reference system to space using abstract words and drawings. For example, we talk about east, west, north, south, up, down, etc. Because math is about assigning order and value to the universe, we tend to do it directionally. Another illustration: We write small to large numbers from left to right. To read a map, one must have a reference for space. To find things in your office or desk, there must be an abstract referencing system for space.

Time

A mental model for abstract time (days, minutes, weeks, hours, etc.) is crucial to success in school and work. One way to keep time is emotionally (how it feels), but another is abstractly with a calendar or a clock. Past, present, and future must be in the mental model because, without these, it isn't possible to sequence. Examples of mental models for time would be a timeline, calendar, schedule, or clock.

Part to whole

Part to whole means that one can identify the parts as well as the whole. For example, chapters make a book. Words make a sentence. Writing a term paper has multiple steps. You cannot effectively analyze anything unless you can break it down and understand part to whole.

CANVA

Mental models for content

Another critical piece of achievement is content comprehension. Just as reading comprehension means you understand the reading passage, content comprehension means you understand the content at a level that you can manipulate it and use it.

To use and manipulate content, in addition to knowing the meaning of vocabulary, you also must know the purpose, structures, patterns, and processes used in that particular discipline or content. These four things tell you what is important and not important as you sort information in order to use it.

For example, the purpose of language arts is to study how structure and language are used to influence a reader. It is basically about writers and readers. The structures are the genres (short story, drama, poetry, biography, novel, etc.), grammar, organizational patterns of text, syllables, phonics, etc. The patterns then become units of study. The processes include reading, writing, speaking, filmmaking, and listening. An expert teacher in language arts is going to help students understand that language arts is always about the relationship between the reader and writer—the manipulations of structure, word choice, and organization.

For example, math is about assigning order and value to the universe. We use numbers, space, and time as primary structures to do that. Patterns that are taught include fractions (part to whole of space), decimals (part to whole of numbers), and measurement (assigning the value of space and time). Processes are addition, subtraction, multiplication, and division. An elementary teacher would facilitate a discussion with students about how to know how much space is theirs in a classroom before introducing fractions. The class would measure the room, divide it with masking tape, and calculate space using fractions. The teacher could do the same thing by dividing pizza. The students would then understand why each student needs to know about measurement and fractions.

The purpose of chemistry, in another example, is to understand chemical bonding. The periodic table provides the rules or patterns for bonding. The process used to figure out the bonding is equations. The structure theory has varied from shell theory to vapor cloud theory to string theory.

When the teacher has content comprehension, the teacher spends the majority of the time teaching what is critical to understanding the use and manipulation of the content. For example, in language arts in high school, the teacher doesn't test by asking what color the girl's dress was in the story, but rather: What specific techniques did the writer use to make the reader feel empathetic in relation to the girl? Or how would the reader have felt differently if this short story had been told in the form of a poem?

Lee Shulman found that content comprehension is a critical issue in excellent teaching and, furthermore, that graphic visual representations (mental models) used by the teacher come out of this understanding. He indicated that teachers can then determine when a student has a slight misunderstanding versus no understanding at all.[21]

Quite simply, if the teacher doesn't understand the content against these four criteria—purpose, structures, patterns, and processes—the teacher will have difficulty facilitating or developing high achievement. It isn't possible to teach what you don't know.

The processes (how)

To do any task requires a "how" component that is the process. Unless the "how" is directly taught, a student doesn't have a key tool for completing the task. One of the reasons generic study skills have not been as successful as the researchers would like is that processes are specific to tasks.

Some "how" approaches/strategies include:

1. Use planning behaviors.
2. Focus perception on a specific stimulus.
3. Control impulsivity.
4. Explore data systematically.
5. Use appropriate and accurate labels.
6. Organize space using stable systems of reference.
7. Orient data in time.
8. Identify constancies across variations.
9. Gather precise and accurate data.
10. Consider two sources of information at once.
11. Organize data (parts of a whole).
12. Visually transport data.

Another cognitive process is question making

Question making has a huge payoff in learning. Question making is the tool that allows you to get inside your brain and know what you know and what you don't know. When students say to you, "I don't understand," and you ask them what part they don't understand, and they say, "all of it," then you know the students don't know how to ask questions syntactically. The good news is that question making can be taught.

A quick approach is to give students the question stems and then have them use the rules to develop a multiple-choice question. Creating multiple-choice questions develops critical thinking skills.

Abstract realities of technology

Negotiating technology is not for the faint of heart. Each year, it becomes more and more complex, particularly with the amount of cybercrime, online bullying, human trafficking, artificial intelligence, etc.

One of the misunderstandings about students from survival and homelessness is that because they play video games and have a cell phone, they understand the technology demands of school. They don't. Many have never had their own computer, do not know basic software (unless taught at school, and if they are homeless, they probably missed a lot of that instruction) behind documents, do not know how to upload files, don't know how to keep security protocols, etc. Word, Excel, and PowerPoint documents, and similar, are the digital version of paper documents. They have to be learned.

Strategies

The book *Research-Based Strategies* (visit www.ahaprocess.com for more information) is full of strategies for abstract representational systems. These strategies are tied to John Hattie's research on effect size.[22]

Summary

1. Many students become disengaged from school because of the abstract representational reality of the content.
2. Language is key in negotiation of your context.
3. Conflict resolution requires appropriate voice and staying out of the Karpman triangle.
4. Mental models translate the concrete sensory to the abstract.
5. There are generic and content-based mental models.
6. Abstract processes, such as planning, are necessary for school.
7. The abstract applications of the digital world must be directly taught.

CHAPTER 7

CHANGING YOUR STORY FROM DISENGAGEMENT TO CHOICE AND CONNECTION IN YOUR CONTEXT

"Stories about self, the world, and relationships are based in autonomic state."[23] —Deb Dana

Is your story one of connection, protection, or disengagement/disappearance?

Metaphor Story
A Hole in Your Heart

by Rubén Perez

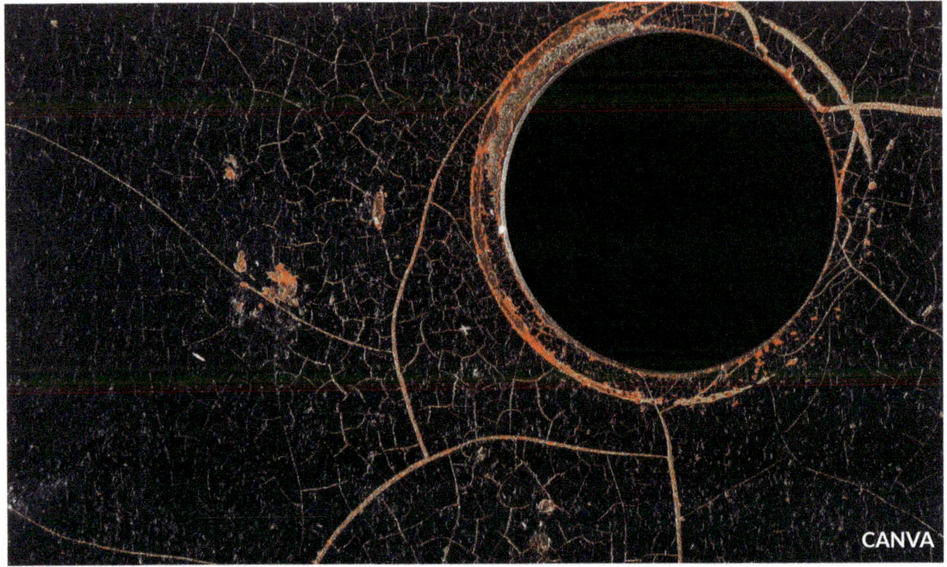

"I love this story by Rubén Perez. Where you have a 'hole in your heart' is where your shame is, and it is where you work to fill that hole in your heart."
—Ruby Payne

During my third year of teaching, I was faced with the dilemma of having to deal with the reality that we had a kleptomaniac loose in our elementary school. I was certain it was not one of my students as I felt I had a good grasp of what occurred in my immediate circle. We were in the middle of the school year when the pattern of missing items gained momentum. It started with one or two missing items a week and progressed to an almost daily occurrence within a month. Pencils, erasers, rulers, and various other personal items were disappearing, slowly at first and then much more rapidly as the year progressed. At some point my students started to accept it as normal, and even more tragically, expected. When we returned from recess or transitional classes, students would do an immediate desk check and announce what was missing. Comments like, "Well, whoever it is got my ruler," "Yeah, my new pencil is missing," and "I don't leave anything in my desk anymore; I take everything with me because I know somebody is going to steal something" were becoming more frequent.

My frustration level over this reality was extremely high. I just could not understand how this person could not be caught in a time period spanning about four weeks. On a day when my students were in music class, the principal called a last-minute meeting for our fifth-grade team. I ran to my classroom to get a folder where I kept notes for every meeting we held. As I walked in, I saw a student of mine named Sammy on his knees, quietly sifting through the contents of a desk in the middle of the classroom. I was so focused on getting my folder that it took me a minute to realize he was not at his assigned desk; he was at someone else's desk. It was at this moment that I stopped and looked at him. He was red-faced and staring back at me. I knew him to be reserved, timid, and sensitive. He was the kind of child whose shy mannerisms could easily make him invisible in a crowd.

"Sammy, it's you?"

He replied "yes" in a whisper and stood there motionless. With purposeful and directive delivery, I asked him to put back everything he had just taken and return to music class, and I informed him we now had an appointment to have lunch together the next day. His shame-filled demeanor led me to believe I had little to worry about between that moment and our scheduled conversation.

It was during our talk that I asked all the typical questions most people would ask: "Why have you been taking other people's property? Weren't you afraid of getting caught? Don't you know that this type of behavior will only lead to worse problems?"

I felt increasingly defeated as Sammy gave answers that didn't help the situation. He kept responding with noncommittal and ill-focused answers that were laced with enough guilt and shame to prevent us from having a meaningful conversation. "I don't know," he would say, or, "Yeah, I know." Despite the shallowness and choppy nature of our conversation, Sammy's nonverbals were communicating something I didn't fully understand. I proceeded with a gut feeling.

"Sammy, is there someone in your life who calls you stupid?" That is when his eyes locked onto mine.

"Yes."

"Who is it?"

"My mom."

I instantly and instinctively regretted asking the question. How in the world could I possibly address Sammy being called stupid by his mother without diminishing her in his eyes? I needed to advocate for Sammy, but I also felt the weight of having to advocate for the relationship he had with his mother.

"I have a question, Sammy. When your mother calls you stupid, is she ever in a good mood? Does she only say that word when she is stressed or angry?"

His facial expression told me that he was deep in thought and trying to be as honest as possible. "She only says it when she's angry."

I said, "I'm not going to defend anyone for calling you stupid. It's wrong and it's hurtful. What I will say is this: The fact that your mother does not call you stupid when she is in a good mood and when things are going well is your proof that she really does love you. I've met your mother, and I know a little bit of what goes on in her life. She has three jobs, and I can only imagine the amount of stress she is under on a daily basis. She is working very hard to keep a home and pay the bills. When people are angry or stressed, they sometimes yell at the people they love the most. I don't know why that is, but it's the people we believe will never run away from us who often get the harshest treatment. It's not that your mother thinks you're stupid. It's that she is so frustrated that she takes her anger out on people at home, away from the people who affect her job. But that part doesn't help you at all. It just hurts regardless of why it happens. By the looks of things, it hurts pretty deeply.

"Do you know what a black hole is?" I asked. We had already established ourselves as huge Star Wars fans, and Sammy was particularly interested in space.

"Of course," he said. "It's a hole in space that has superpower suction. It is so strong it even absorbs light."

"That's correct. It is so strong that it takes in anything around it. When our hearts carry a hurt, it can sometimes feel like our hearts have a black hole. Hearts can get so hurt and so empty that it can make us feel a sense of urgency to fill it with something. Black holes don't care what you fill them with; they are hungry for anything that is close to them.

"Here is what I suspect might be happening, Sammy. When you take things, it feels exciting. Sometimes, there is a little bit of an adrenaline rush when we break rules and try not to get caught. When you take things, the excitement can make it feel like you are putting something in the black hole of your heart."

While I was saying this, I also mimed the actions of grabbing things for visual purposes. I slowly grabbed pencils, markers, tape rolls, etc., and placed them inside my shirt, where I kept them pressed against my heart. The visual caught his attention.

"The problem is that the excitement does not last very long. So, you do it again. Then again and again. Pretty soon, you have a habit of taking things just to feel the excitement. Sammy, a black hole never gets full. You must deal with the reason it exists first. No ruler or pencil will ever fill the hurt."

He was quiet for a while. He affirmed that what I demonstrated was very similar to his experience. We spoke a bit more before I felt it was time to address his actions.

"Sammy, there is a saying that goes: 'Hurt people hurt people.'"

He thought for a minute and replied, "Like my mom sometimes hurts me because she is hurt?"

"Exactly! Now let's talk about how taking people's belongings is a repeat of this cycle."

He immediately recognized the parallel, and there was a strange combination of guilt and relief on his face. I surmised that he finally understood why he did what he did. He didn't want to hurt other people; he was not focused on that part of the equation. After he admitted full responsibility for his actions, he agreed to return all the items he had taken. Two weeks later, Sammy approached me and said that ever since our conversation, he had stopped stealing. More significantly, he had also stopped having the need to steal as well. We did not have an issue with missing items for the rest of the school year.

Sammy was not, in any way, shape, or form, a bad kid. He was a hurt kid whose actions hurt others while he was trying to cope with his own pain. I did not excuse his actions, nor did I minimize the offense of theft. My assessment was that Sammy's emotional wound needed attention first. Only then would he be able to take his eyes off himself to see how his actions affected others. It was so gratifying to see him accept full responsibility and start making decisions based on a deeper level of empathy for himself and his classmates.

Where do you get your story?

You don't do it by yourself. "Narrative ecology of self" refers to a compilation of stories that a person hears and sees (and sometimes is not told), the stories others tell of that person, and the social context of the stories. This is McLean's model of narrative ecology of self:[24]

McLean's model of narrative ecology of self

Identity is held in the stories we tell ourselves about ourselves, in the stories others tell about us, and in the stories our culture tells.

Source: *The Coauthored Self* by K. McLean

We get the stories of who we are from multiple sources, and so often we are not aware of that, as was the case in the above story. These stories then impact our ANS and make a huge impact on where we are on the hierarchy. What fires together wires together. If we have had multiple negative experiences with our family, at school, at work, with friends, etc., then as we enter that environment, those stories resurface and impact whether we think we have connection, need protection, or disengage.

Toxic co-authors and toxic situations need to be addressed. One way to take away the power of a toxic co-author is to relive a situation in which you had an encounter and then simply, in your mind, remove that person and put a person who loves you in that space. Then ask yourself, What would they (the person who loves you) have said had they been there? You will realize that the story was dependent upon who was in the room and had very little to do with you.

These are in our stories:

- One thing I am good at is...
- One thing I am not good at is...
- Two things that upset me are...
- I don't like it when people...
- Two words that describe me are...
- My parent (mom or dad) says I am...

Key questions

1. Am I mostly in a story of connection? Of protection? Of disengagement?
2. Where am I getting those stories?
3. Do I have toxic co-authors in those stories?
4. Where am I functioning in the hierarchy?
5. Where do I feel safe?
6. Who are the toxic co-authors from whom I need to separate myself?

Strategies

1. Metaphor story
2. Identifying toxic co-authors
3. Creating a future story
4. Changing where we operate on the hierarchy (Deb Dana's book *Polyvagal Exercises for Safety and Connection* has many strategies in it for moving up the hierarchy)

Summary

1. The ANS significantly impacts the story we carry around in our head about ourselves and the world.
2. We can manage the hierarchy to make that happen.

We can provide this information to our students.

CONCLUSION

HOW TO IMPLEMENT THE IDEAS IN THIS BOOK

As we better understand the autonomic nervous system of the body, we can increase learning, stabilize resources, and move to a greater level of connection. We can negotiate the hierarchy and choose to have the story of connection as much as possible. We can help our students achieve that story as well.

I asked Vern Reed, a practicing educator for many years, to write an implementation guide for teachers and administrators. That extensive (and free) resource may be found at **www.ahaprocess.com/disengaged**. Vern also offers some words below.

Implementation Guide

From Vern Reed:

There is no question that the information outlined in this book can and will help teachers and administrators who work with under-resourced students and students who are experiencing homelessness. However, the key is how you and your school intentionally implement the information and processes.

Dr. Payne offers tools and strategies at the end of each chapter, but she also wants to make sure that each reader has a great understanding of what classroom or school-wide implementation might look like.

The implementation guide addresses this concern. It takes the learning from chapters 1–6 and offers step-by-step ideas for educators. The final piece of the guide is for administrators, and it offers several ways to implement these ideas in a school or a district. These are not the only ways the learning can be used, but they do represent examples that have already been utilized by educators and administrators.

We hope that the ideas offered in this book help you in your efforts to connect with under-resourced students and students who are experiencing homelessness.

APPENDIX

A little quiz

You are invited to take the following three-part quiz, adapted from Payne's *A Framework for Understanding Poverty*. Put a check mark by all the things you know how to do.

Could you survive in poverty?

Please remember that there are differences between rural and urban poverty, particularly regarding transportation. Also, there are differences in generational and situational/working poverty. (Thank you to Sonia Bond-Holycross for the updates.)

Put a check by each item that applies to you.

- ☐ I know how to live without utilities and a phone.
- ☐ I carry or have access to self-defense instruments like pepper spray, pocketknives, tasers, and/or guns and am willing to use them.
- ☐ I can entertain a group of friends with my personality and my stories.
- ☐ I know how to use money transfer apps like Cash App and platforms like OnlyFans as employment.
- ☐ I know which churches will provide assistance with shelter. I know what to say to get a church to "go the extra mile" for me. I know which agencies in my town will help with certain resources and how much they will help.
- ☐ I know how to move in half a day and in the middle of the night. I know where people experiencing homelessness live in my town (often tent cities).
- ☐ I know how to get and use electronic benefits for food.
- ☐ I often find myself without my personal documents, and I know which agencies can provide me with a copy of my personal documents if I need them in a pinch.
- ☐ I know where the free medical clinics are. I use the emergency room for most of my medical needs as I don't have access to a general practitioner. I often save a portion of my medication until I need it again or until a family member needs it.

- ☐ I am very good at trading and bartering. I know which things to pick from the trash because they may be worth money.
- ☐ I can get by without a car. I know people who have never had a driver's license and probably never will.
- ☐ I know how to hide my car so it cannot be repossessed. I have traded vehicles with friends to avoid having a car repossessed.
- ☐ I own pets despite struggling financially to provide for myself and my family.
- ☐ I know which sections of town "belong" to which gangs. I tend to stay in my section of town to shop and live my daily life.
- ☐ There is a neighborhood gas station that allows me to use food stamps for nonfood items.
- ☐ My neighborhood is considered a food desert.

Could you survive in middle class?

Put a check by each item that applies to you.

- ☐ I know how to get my children into sports and sports camps and travel for those events.
- ☐ I use mobile apps to pay bills and track spending and credit card purchases.
- ☐ Each of my children has their own phone, email address, and computer. I have security measures on each device to protect their privacy and security, as well as limit their access to content I do not want them to see.
- ☐ My children know the popular clothing brands and follow influencers on platforms like TikTok.
- ☐ We use Airbnb when we travel, as well as hotels.
- ☐ I know how to use a credit card, checking account, and savings account—and I know what an annuity is. I understand term life insurance, disability insurance, and 80/20 medical insurance, as well as homeowners insurance, flood insurance, and replacement insurance.
- ☐ I talk to my children about getting into college and the levels of competition and preparation necessary to be accepted by the best colleges.
- ☐ I know how to get a good interest rate on the loan for my new car.

- ☐ I understand the difference among the principal, interest, and escrow statements on my house payment.
- ☐ I know how to help my children with their homework, I use online resources for help, and I don't hesitate to call the school if I need additional information.
- ☐ I know how to decorate the house for the different holidays.
- ☐ I and/or my family belong to an athletic/exercise club or have a Peloton.
- ☐ We have a computer for each member of the household, high speed Internet access, and hotspots.
- ☐ I repair items in my house almost immediately when they break—or know a repair service and call it.
- ☐ We have accounts with multiple social media platforms.
- ☐ We plan our vacations six months to a year in advance.
- ☐ I contribute to a retirement plan separate from Social Security.
- ☐ I am billed for subscriptions to various streaming services.

Could you survive in wealth?

Please note that the wealthiest 1% of households starts with those that have a net worth of around $10 million but also includes households whose net worth is in the billions. There is a great deal of variation in this continuum.

Put a check by each item that applies to you.

- ☐ I can read a menu in at least three languages.
- ☐ I have several favorite restaurants in different countries. I host dinner parties at my residences because my private chef is superb and the selection of wines, spirits, and cocktails is much better than the best restaurants have.
- ☐ During the holidays, I hire a decorator to identify the appropriate themes and items with which to decorate the house.
- ☐ I have a preferred financial adviser, legal firm, certified public accounting firm, designer, florist, caterer, domestic employment service, and hairdresser. In addition, I have a preferred tailor/designer, jeweler, travel agency, and personal trainer. I have a personal shopper who selects clothes for me for each upcoming fashion season and ensures that no one in my social set has purchased the same clothes.

- ☐ I have at least two residences that are staffed and maintained.
- ☐ I know how to ensure confidentiality and loyalty from my domestic staff.
- ☐ I have several layers of security that keep people whom I do not wish to see away from me.
- ☐ I fly privately in my own plane or the company plane, or sometimes first class on an international flight.
- ☐ My children are enrolled in the preferred private schools and have a nanny. I select personal tutors and sports trainers who have acknowledged expertise and, often, name recognition.
- ☐ I host the parties that "key" people attend.
- ☐ I am on the boards of at least two charities and one company that is publicly traded.
- ☐ I contribute to at least four or five political campaigns.
- ☐ I support or buy the work of particular artists.
- ☐ I know how to read a corporate financial statement and analyze my own financial statements.
- ☐ I belong to two or three private clubs (country club, yacht club, etc.) and carefully scrutinize my bill each month.
- ☐ I own multiple vehicles, often titled in a name other than my own for privacy and litigation reasons.
- ☐ I "buy a table" at several charity events throughout the year.
- ☐ I can cite the provenance (historical documentation) of all my original art, jewelry, antiques, and one-of-a-kind items.
- ☐ My investment portfolio includes stocks, non-fungible tokens, cryptocurrency, and gold.
- ☐ I know the differences among superyachts, megayachts, and gigayachts. Two places I like to harbor my yacht are St. Barths and Costa Smeralda, Italy.
- ☐ I have a trust for myself and each of my children. I have a lawyer on retainer.
- ☐ I have a personal public relations/social media specialist who protects and promotes me online.

BIBLIOGRAPHY

Callahan, R., & Trubo, R. (2002). *Tapping the healer within: Using thought-field therapy to instantly conquer your fears, anxieties, and emotional distress.* New York, NY: McGraw-Hill Education.

Clark, R. C. (2008). *Building expertise: Cognitive methods for training and performance improvement.* San Francisco, CA: Pfeiffer.

Dana, D. (2020). *Polyvagal flip chart: Understanding the science of safety.* New York: NY: W. W. Norton & Co.

Haidt, J. (2024). *The anxious generation: How the great rewiring of childhood is causing an epidemic of mental illness.* New York, NY: Penguin Press.

Hattie, J. (2015). The applicability of visible learning to higher education. *Scholarship of Teaching and Learning in Psychology*, 1, 79–91.

HeartMath Institute (n. d.). A boy and his dog—heart-rhythm entrainment. https://www.heartmath.com/inspire-a-change-of-heart/

Kishiyama, M. M., Boyce, W. T., Jimenez, A. M., Perry, L. M., & Knight, R. T. (2009). Socioeconomic disparities affect prefrontal function in children. *Journal of Cognitive Neuroscience*, 21(6), 1106–1115. doi:10/1162/jocn.2009.21101

McLean, K. C. (2016). *The coauthored self: Family stories and the construction of personal identity.* New York, NY: Oxford University Press.

Mullainathan, S., & Shafir, E. (2013). *Scarcity: The new science of having less and how it defines our lives.* New York, NY: Picador.

Ortner, A. (2016). *Gorilla thumps & bear hugs: A tapping solutions children's story.* Carlsbad, CA: Hay House.

Payne, R. K. (2019). *A framework for understanding poverty* (6th rev. ed.). Highlands, TX: aha! Process.

Porges, S. (2011). *The polyvagal theory: Neurophysiological foundations of emotions, attachment, communication, self-regulation.* New York, NY: W. W. Norton & Co.

School on Wheels. (n. d.). Homelessness in America. https://schoolonwheels.org/homelessness-in- america/

Shulman, L. (1988, November). A union of insufficiencies: Strategies for teacher assessment in a period of educational reform. *Educational Leadership*, 36–41. Retrieved from http://www.ascd.org/ASCD/pdf/journals/ed_lead/el_198811_shulman.pdf

Siegel, D. (2010). *Mindsight: The new science of personal transformation.* New York, NY: Bantam.

Stop Child Homelessness. (n. d.) Meet Rene. https://stopchildhomelessness.org

Stosny, S. (2003). *The powerful self: A workbook for therapeutic self-empowerment*. Germantown, MD: CompassionPower.

Tyng, C. M., Amin, H. U., Saad, M. N. M., & Malik, A. S. (2017). The influences of emotion on learning and memory. *Frontiers in Psychology*, 8, 1454. https://doi.org/10.3389/fpsyg.2017.01454

USAFacts. (2023). What can McKinney–Vento Act data reveal about youth homelessness? https://usafacts.org/articles/what-can-mckinney-vento-act-data-reveal-about-youth-homelessness/#:~:text=High%20school%20graduation%20rates%20among,long%2Dterm%20disadvantages%-¬20without%20support

ENDNOTES

[1] C. M. Tyng et al., "The Influences of Emotion on Learning and Memory"

[2] S. Porges, *The Polyvagal Theory*

[3] HeartMath Institute, "A Boy and His Dog—Heart-Rhythm Entrainment"

[4] D. Dana, *Polyvagal Flip Chart*

[5] S. Porges, *The Polyvagal Theory*

[6] R. K. Payne, *A Framework for Understanding Poverty*

[7] R. C. Clark, *Building Expertise*

[8] D. Siegel, *Mindsight*, page 18

[9] *Ibid.*, pages 18–19

[10] *Ibid.*, page 19

[11] M. M. Kishiyama et al., "Socioeconomic Disparities Affect Prefrontal Function in Children"

[12] D. Siegel, *Mindsight*, page 26

[13] S. Stosny, *The Powerful Self*

[14] D. Siegel, *Mindsight*, page 26

[15] R. Callahan & R. Trubo, *Tapping the Healer Within*; A. Ortner, *Gorilla Thumps & Bear Hugs*

[16] J. Haidt, *The Anxious Generation*

[17] S. Mullainathan & E. Shafir, *Scarcity*

[18] USAFacts, "What can McKinney–Vento Act data reveal about youth homelessness?"

[19] School on Wheels, "Homelessness in America"

[20] Stop Child Homelessness, "Meet Rene"

[21] L. Shulman, "A Union of Insufficiencies"

[22] J. Hattie, "The Applicability of Visible Learning to Higher Education"

[23] D. Dana, *Polyvagal Flip Chart*

[24] K. McLean, *The Coauthored Self*

ABOUT THE AUTHOR

Ruby K. Payne, Ph.D. is CEO and founder of aha! Process and an author, speaker, publisher, and career educator. She is a leading expert on the mindsets of economic class and on crossing socioeconomic lines in education and work. Payne is recognized internationally for her foundational and award-winning book, *A Framework for Understanding Poverty*, now in its sixth edition, which has sold more than 1.8 million copies. Payne has helped students and adults of all economic backgrounds achieve academic, professional, and personal success.

Payne's expertise stems from more than 30 years of experience in public schools. She has traveled extensively and has presented her work throughout North America and in Europe, Australia, China, and India. She has spoken to more than 2 million educators and trained more than 7,000 trainers to do her work. Her speaking engagements have included EARCOS (East Asia Regional Council of Schools) in Malaysia, National Association of School Boards, Central States Bankers Conference, Federal Reserve Board of Governors, Beijing Institute of Education, Harvard Summer Institute for Principals, as well as thousands of individual school districts and campuses.

Payne has written or co-authored more than a dozen books. Recent publications are the popular and award-winning *Emotional Poverty in All Demographics*, *Emotional Poverty, Volume 2*, and *Navigating Emotional Realities with Adults: Emotional Poverty at Work*, as well as the digital (and free) *Before You Quit Teaching*, which won the Independent Publisher Book Awards gold medal for an adult informational ebook.

Payne received a bachelor's degree from Goshen College, a master's degree in English Literature from Western Michigan University, and a Ph.D. in Educational Leadership and Policy from Loyola University Chicago.

- **Visit ahaprocess.com for free resources: articles, video clips, and success stories from practitioners—and read our aha! Moments blog!**
- **Sign up for our latest LIVE online workshop offerings at ahaprocess.com/events:**
  - Emotional Poverty workshop AND Trainer Certification
  - Bridges Across Every Divide
  - Getting Ahead in a Just-Gettin'-By World
  - Bridges Out of Poverty workshop AND Trainer Certification
  - Tactical Communication
  - Research-Based Strategies
- **Register for on-demand workshops at ahaprocess.com/on-demand**
- **If you like *Educating Students Experiencing Homelessness, Instability, and Disengagement,* check out these publications:**
  - *Emotional Poverty in All Demographics: How to Reduce Anger, Anxiety, and Violence in the Classroom* (Payne)
  - *Emotional Poverty Volume 2: Safer Students and Less-Stressed Teachers* (Payne)
  - *A Framework for Understanding Poverty: A Cognitive Approach, 6th Edition* (Payne)
  - *Research-Based Strategies: Narrowing the Achievement Gap for Under-Resourced Students* (Payne & Tucker)
  - *Bridges Across Every Divide: Policy and Practices to Reduce Poverty and Build Communities* (DeVol & Krebs)
  - *Workplace Stability: Creating Conditions That Lead to Retention, Productivity, and Engagement in Entry-Level Workers* (Weirich)
- **Connect with us on Facebook, X, and Instagram—and watch our YouTube channel**

For a complete listing of products, please visit ahaprocess.com

Join us on Facebook
facebook.com/rubypayne
facebook.com/bridgesoutofpoverty

X
@ahaprocess
#AddressPoverty
#BridgesOutofPoverty

Subscribe to our YouTube channel
youtube.com/ahaprocess

Read our blog
ahaprocess.com/blog

Instagram
@ahaprocess

TikTok
@rubykpayne